Natalie Babbitt

Twayne's United States Authors Series
Children's Literature

Ruth K. MacDonald, Editor

TUSAS 573

NATALIE BABBITT
Photograph courtesy of the estate of Thomas Victor, by permission of Harriet Spurlin.

Natalie Babbitt

Michael M. Levy
University of Wisconsin–Stout

Twayne Publishers • Boston
A Division of G. K. Hall & Co.

813
B11zL

Natalie Babbitt
Michael M. Levy

Copyright 1991 by G. K. Hall & Co.
All rights reserved.
Published by Twayne Publishers
A Division of G. K. Hall & Co.
70 Lincoln Street
Boston, Massachusetts 02111

Copyediting supervised by Barbara Sutton.
Book production by Janet Z. Reynolds.
Typeset by Compset, Inc., Beverly, Massachusetts.

10 9 8 7 6 5 4 3 2 1

Library of Congress Cataloging-in-Publication Data

Levy, Michael M.
    Natalie Babbitt / Michael M. Levy.
       p. cm.—(Twayne's United States authors series ; TUSAS
  573. Children's literature)
    Includes bibliographical references and index.
    ISBN 0-8057-7612-5 (alk. paper)
    1. Babbitt, Natalie—Criticism and interpretation.   2. Children's
stories, American—History and criticism. I. Title. II. Series:
Twayne's United States authors series ; TUSAS 573. III. Series:
Twayne's United States authors series. Children's literature.
PS3552.A1735Z78   1991
813′ .54—dc20
                                                    90-48065

To Sandy, Scott, and Miriam Anne

Contents

Preface

When I was first asked to write on Natalie Babbitt's work I was familiar with *Tuck Everlasting,* her generally acknowledged masterpiece, and *The Devil's Storybook,* but had not yet read any of her other fiction. Perhaps the greatest pleasure of preparing to write this volume, therefore, was becoming familiar with the author's entire body of work. Reading Babbitt's books in the order in which they were published, I quickly gained an appreciation of her development as a writer. The early picture books, I realized, were, in so far as their texts were concerned, well done but essentially lightweight exercises. Babbitt already felt fairly comfortable with herself as an illustrator, and in *Dick Foote and the Shark* (1967) and *Phoebe's Revolt* (1968) she used verse as a kind of prop—she, with her insistence on honesty, might even call it a crutch—to give herself the courage to tell simple stories. In *The Search for Delicious* (1969) she was ready to try something more difficult, a novel, and she succeeded delightfully. Even *Delicious,* however, although an enjoyable romp with a satisfying message, is nothing extraordinary. With each work that followed, I discovered, Babbitt showed herself ready to try something new, something more difficult. *Kneeknock Rise* (1970), *Goody Hall* (1971), and *The Devil's Storybook* (1974) were all more ambitious than *The Search for Delicious,* their themes more complex, the demands they made on their audiences more sophisticated. They in turn were cast into partial shadow by the artistic success and telling moral ambiguity of *Tuck Everlasting* (1975) and *The Eyes of the Amaryllis* (1977). Then, in 1982, Babbitt published *Herbert Rowbarge,* a deeply ironic and heavily mythic novel that was clearly aimed at adults.

It occurred to me that with only one exception, the picture book *The Something* (1970), Babbitt's fiction could be seen as spanning a clear continuum from less sophisticated to more sophisticated, from books aimed at a younger audience to books appropriate for an older audience, almost as if she were writing for a specific child or children, her own perhaps, who were growing up. I also began to notice in her work reoccurring images, themes, motifs: the child orphaned or isolated from his or her parents, the adult obsessed with material wealth and prestige, bodies of water asked to carry a heavy symbolic freight, memories and the difficulty of coming to terms with the past, a run of almost Shakespearean wise fools.

The organization of the text is primarily chronological. Following a detailed biographical chapter is a discussion of Babbitt's early work as an illustrator and author, starting with her illustration of the picture book *The Forty-Ninth Magician* (1966), written by her husband Samuel Babbitt, and continuing with her own early picture books *Dick Foote and the Shark* and *Phoebe's Revolt.* Chapter 3 discusses Babbitt's first two novels, *The Search for Delicious* and *Kneeknock Rise,* and argues that both books center on the difficult discovery, made by all children at some point, that adults are not all-wise and all-knowing. Chapter 4 points out how *The Something* and *Goody Hall* are, in part, demonstrations of how children learn to deal with their deepest and darkest fears. In *Goody Hall* Babbitt continues her examination of how children cope with the discovery of their parents' fallibility. Chapter 5 forsakes strict chronological order to discuss Babbitt's interrelated short story collections, *The Devil's Storybook* and *The Devil's Other Storybook* (1987). Chapters 6 and 7 concentrate on the author's two most sophisticated novels for children, *Tuck Everlasting* and *The Eyes of the Amaryllis,* arguing that in these two books Babbitt has begun seriously to modify the optimism, the belief in unadulterated happy endings, that was virtually a trademark in her earlier fiction. Chapter 8 examines *Herbert Rowbarge* and demonstrates that the book is indeed a novel for adults and that it has to some extent been undervalued by reviewers who haven't understood either its intended audience or its deeply ironic nature. A concluding chapter discusses Babbitt's current writing and illustrating projects, some of which may be published before this volume becomes available. The final chapter also places Natalie Babbitt and her work within the context of contemporary children's literature.

It is necessary here to mention the enormous help that Natalie Babbitt has been in the preparation of this book. She not only responded to my first inquiry, but to a whole series of later letters, giving detailed answers and sending me copies of unpublished speeches, galley proofs, and essays. Most important, she played gracious host to me and my family at her Cape Cod summer house in August 1987 and spent nearly eight hours talking to me about her books and her life. This volume could, perhaps, have been written without her help, but it would not have been anywhere near as complete.

I would also like to acknowledge the enormous help I have received in writing this book from two other people. First, my wife, Sandra Lindow, who has always been my most demanding reader and critic. Second, my colleague and friend, Virginia L. Wolf, who taught me the majority of what I know about children's literature.

Acknowledgments

Excerpts from the following books are reprinted by permission of Farrar, Straus & Giroux, Inc.

The Devil's Storybook by Natalie Babbitt. © 1974 by Natalie Babbitt.

The Devil's Other Storybook by Natalie Babbitt. © 1987 by Natalie Babbitt.

Dick Foote and the Shark by Natalie Babbitt. © 1967 by Natalie Babbitt.

The Eyes of the Amaryllis by Natalie Babbitt. © 1977 by Natalie Babbitt.

Goody Hall by Natalie Babbitt. © 1971 by Natalie Babbitt.

Herbert Rowbarge by Natalie Babbitt. © 1982 by Natalie Babbitt.

Kneeknock Rise by Natalie Babbitt. © 1970 by Natalie Babbitt.

Phoebe's Revolt by Natalie Babbitt. © 1968 by Natalie Babbitt.

The Search for Delicious by Natalie Babbitt. © 1969 by Natalie Babbitt.

The Something by Natalie Babbitt. © 1970 by Natalie Babbitt.

Tuck Everlasting by Natalie Babbitt. © 1975 by Natalie Babbitt.

Chronology

1932   Natalie Zane Moore born 28 July in Dayton, Ohio, to Ralph Zane Moore, a business administrator, and Genevieve (Converse) Moore.

1933   Father loses job as a result of the Great Depression, and family moves to Indian Lake, future setting of *Herbert Rowbarge*.

1935   Family moves to Westerville, Ohio, a suburb of Columbus. Mother persuaded by peer pressure not to pursue a career in art.

1938   Family moves to Middletown, Ohio, and Natalie starts first grade.

1944   Father takes a government job, and family moves to Willowick, Ohio, a suburb of Cleveland. Natalie sees Lake Erie for the first time, a major influence on *The Eyes of the Amaryllis*.

1947   Enters the Laurel School for Girls, Cleveland.

1948   Family moves to Shaker Heights, Ohio.

1950   Enters Smith College, Northampton, Massachusetts, as a theater major, but quickly switches to studio art.

1952   Meets Samuel Babbitt, then a junior at Yale.

1954   Graduates with a B.A. from Smith College. Marries Samuel Babbitt on June 26. Moves to New Haven, Connecticut. Samuel takes job as administrator at Yale.

1956   First child, Christopher, is born. Natalie's mother dies.

1957   Samuel takes job as dean of men at Vanderbilt University. Family moves to Nashville, Tennessee.

1958 Second child, Thomas, is born.

1960 Third child, Lucy, is born.

1962 Samuel takes administrative job with the Peace Corps. Family moves to Washington, D.C.

1964 Reads Betty Friedan's *The Feminine Mystique.*

1966 Illustrates her husband's children's book, *The Forty-ninth Magician,* her first professional sale. Samuel becomes president of the newly founded Kirkland College in Clinton, New York. The family builds a house in the Adirondack foothills, later to be the setting of *Tuck Everlasting.*

1967 *Dick Foote and the Shark.* Chosen a Junior Literary Guild Selection, the first of many such honors.

1968 *Phoebe's Revolt.*

1969 *The Search for Delicious.* Chosen as the best book of 1969 for children ages nine to twelve by the *New York Times.* Natalie begins to teach writing and illustrating for children at Kirkland College.

1970 *Kneeknock Rise* and *The Something. Kneeknock Rise* chosen a Newbery Honor Book.

1971 *Goody Hall.*

1972 Illustrates *Small Poems* by Valerie Worth, the beginning of an ongoing collaboration.

1974 *The Devil's Storybook.* Nominated for the National Book Award.

1975 *Tuck Everlasting,* Natalie's most famous novel.

1976 *Tuck Everlasting* receives the Christopher Award.

1977 *The Eyes of the Amaryllis.*

1978 Kirkland College merges with Hamilton College, and the Babbitts spend the year on Cape Cod.

1979 Natalie receives the George G. Stone Award for her work in children's literature. Samuel takes a job as vice president of Memorial Sloan-Kettering Cancer Center. The Babbitts move to an apartment in New York but buy a home on Cape Cod.

1982 *Herbert Rowbarge.*

1983 Samuel takes a job as vice-president of Brown University. Babbitts move to Providence, Rhode Island.

1987 *The Devil's Other Storybook.*

1988 Peter Sargent Frattaroli, Natalie's first grandchild, is born to her daughter, the novelist Lucy Cullyford Babbitt.

1989 *Nellie—a Cat on Her Own,* Natalie's first full-color picture book. Is a finalist for the Laura Ingalls Wilder Medal of the American Library Association (nomination recognizes her life's work in children's literature).

1

Life as a History of Moving

Ancestry and Early Life

Born Natalie Zane Moore on 28 July 1932 in Dayton, Ohio, the daughter of Ralph Zane Moore and Genevieve Converse Moore, Babbitt is descended through both parents from settlers who came to America from England in the 1600s.[1] Two of her father's ancestors, Philip and Conrad Moore, founded what is now Moorefield, West Virginia, seat of sparsely populated Hardy County in the state's Eastern Panhandle, the site of the town having been surveyed by George Washington. On the other side, her father's Zane ancestors pioneered in the Ohio River Valley in what Babbitt has referred to as "the most romantic kind of way" (autobiographical essay, 1). Zanesville, Ohio, bears their name, as does the Zane's Trace Wilderness Trail. In the early 1770s two of the Zanes, Isaac and Jonathan, were kidnapped by the Wyandotte Indians as children and were taken north to what is now Detroit, Michigan. Babbitt recounts that Jonathan was released two years later, but that Isaac "stayed, married Myeerah, the chief's daughter, and was later given credit for keeping the Wyandottes loyal to the American side during the Revolution"(2). He also gained the appellation "the White Eagle of the Wyandottes." It may be that these events are echoed, if faintly, in *Tuck Everlasting* by the

1

kidnapping of Winnie Foster and her near marriage to Jesse
Tuck. Meanwhile, Ebenezer Zane, a brother of Isaac and Jonathan, had also joined the fight for independence. Ebenezer com-
manded Fort Fincastle (later Fort Henry), site of one of the last
battles of the war in September 1782. The fort, which eventually
became the location of Wheeling, West Virginia, was also home to
the Zane boys' sister, Betty, who herself gained fame for carrying
gunpowder to the defenders of the fort in her apron.

Babbitt's maternal ancestors, the Converses, first settled in
New England in the 1630s. Later they too moved to Ohio and
began founding towns. George Leroy Converse, for example, was
one of several founders of Columbus, Ohio. The Reverend Jere-
miah Converse was the first settler in Darby, later Plain City,
Ohio. The family also fought in the Revolution. A close relative,
Zebulon Pike, was an officer in the War of 1812 and later went
out to Colorado and discovered Pike's Peak.

Babbitt reports that, although her mother was proud of Zebulon Pike, "she always felt that the branch of the Converses who
stayed in the East was the really distinguished branch" (autobiographical essay, 2). It is only human nature to want to think of
oneself as having ancestors of some importance, but it seems
clear that Genevieve Moore's interest in her roots went well beyond mere genealogical curiosity and became something of an obsession with what she saw as her family's genteel past. Although
she was born and lived virtually her entire life in Ohio, she spoke
regularly of her desire to "move back" to New England, a place
she had never actually lived. This desire was so strong in her
that, many years later, in accordance with her mother's wishes,
Babbitt "sprinkled her ashes on a Connecticut hillside, which
brought her home at last" (2). Genevieve Moore's belief in her
family's innate or at least ancestral gentility was clearly a major
early influence on her daughter and became a reoccurring element in many of Babbitt's novels, particularly *Goody Hall, Tuck
Everlasting,* and *Herbert Rowbarge.*

Babbitt insists that, after the Revolution, with the exception of
Zebulon Pike, her ancestors on both sides did very little that was
extraordinary. For the most part, they settled down and became

farmers, teachers, and, in a few cases, ministers, though her paternal grandfather, Opha Moore, was private secretary to four governors of Ohio, including William McKinley. Babbitt writes that when McKinley "wanted to take my grandfather with him when he was elected President . . . my grandmother didn't want to leave Columbus, which underscores my statement about the Zanes not doing much after the Revolution" (autobiographical essay, 3).

Natalie's father, Ralph Moore, was born in Columbus, Ohio, in 1893 and died in 1970. Natalie's mother, Genevieve Converse, was born in Martins Ferry, Ohio, in 1902 and died in 1956, when Babbitt was only twenty-four. Her parents first met in Columbus and were married there on 16 June 1928. Ralph was a widower and had a daughter by his first marriage. Ralph and Genevieve both had experience as teachers, he of math and shop, she of art, though by the time they met Ralph had switched to the field of industrial relations, working for General Motors. Natalie's older sister Diane was born in Dayton in 1930. Natalie followed twenty-four months later.

A key event in Babbitt's life occurred in January 1933 when she was six months old and her sister Diane was two. The Great Depression was at its height and her father, through no fault of his own, lost his job. The family also had to give up their house in Dayton, Ohio, the only home they were ever to own. Fortunately, Genevieve's mother owned a cottage at Russells Point, a small town on Indian Lake, part way between Lima and Columbus in northwest Ohio, and the Moores moved there immediately. Babbitt's parents told her that her father spent most of the next year fishing and looking for a job, while her mother "began what she always claimed was the delicious and absorbing task of raising two daughters" (autobiographical essay, 1).

Although Babbitt has few first hand memories of this early period of her life, the more than two years that she spent in the cottage at Russells Point seem to have had a strong effect on her development both as a person and as a writer. The south shore of Indian Lake was and is a beautiful place, the site of a small amusement park and, some years later, a state park. Clearly a symbol of tranquillity to Babbitt—although sometimes tranquillity under attack from outside forces—Indian Lake appears in various forms again and again in her fiction. There is, for example, the mermaid's lake in Babbitt's first novel, *The Search for Delicious*, which becomes the key to the health of an entire kingdom, and there is also Tuck's pond in *Tuck Everlasting*, beautifully painted by Babbitt for the cover of the current edition of that novel. Most recently, renamed Red Man Lake and transposed to southern Ohio, Indian Lake became the setting for Babbitt's novel *Herbert Rowbarge* (autobiographical essay, 4), the amusement park, which she remembers so vividly, becoming her protagonist's own "Rowbarge Pleasure Dome."

Natalie Babbitt has written that "everything I have turned out to be, for better or worse, seems to be directly traceable to some particular thing that happened before I hit puberty" (autobiograhical essay, 4). She also stated that "my history is a history of moving. Give or take one or two in my infancy, I have lived in twenty-two different houses so far, which works out to something like a new home every two and a half years, on the average" (1), and it seems clear that the many displaced, lonely children of her novels are, in large part, a result of the effect on her of this constant early-childhood shifting from town to town across Ohio. Her father eventually found an industrial relations job with Timken Roller Bearing in Columbus and, in late 1935, moved the family to Westerville, a suburb of the state capital and home of Otterbein College. In the summer of 1938, they moved to Middletown, Ohio, just north of Cincinnati, where Natalie started first grade and where the family joined the decidedly upper-class Episcopal church. She reports that "this move was, I see in retrospect, a difficult one for me. I lost my appetite and wasn't hungry for the next six years, which earned me the nickname 'the human skeleton.' " It was at this time, too, that Babbitt developed "a deep anxiety about being alone in strange places that has plagued me all my life" (7), an anxiety that she shares with many of her characters, particularly Egan in *Kneeknock Rise*, Winnie in *Tuck Everlasting*, and Jenny in *The Eyes of the Amaryllis*, all of whom find themselves unhappily far from home. Despite this anxiety and a propensity to write numbers backwards, which Babbitt attributes to being lefthanded, she was a good student, learned to read quickly, and developed an immediate love for fairytales and myths. She and her mother also shared a taste for anagrams, and she did a lot of drawing. Fortunately, her father was working for a company that made paper, and he took to bringing home piles of it, culled from the company's reject bins.

Like many authors of fiction for young people, Natalie Babbitt seems to be in very close touch with her childhood—she has written that she remembers it "vividly"[2]—and her essays and speeches are replete with telling anecdotes about her childhood adventures. As with any attempt to recount events long past, the exact accuracy of her stories may be suspect, but from those stories emerges the picture of a strong-willed, skinny, serious little girl, with a well-developed sense of right and wrong and an exceedingly whimsical imagination. In a speech entitled "Moral Dilemmas and Doll Underwear," for example, Babbitt describes a series of encounters with other children that, she believes, gave her important insights into the world around her. She recalls at the age of three watching Mildred Mendenhall, the four-year-old daughter of the Lutheran minister, steal her sister Diane's doll underwear. "My sister and I went home . . . and complained loudly to our mother about the theft. But it seemed there was nothing to be done. Our mother, feisty as she was about most things, couldn't quite bring herself to cross the yard and confront the Reverend Dr. Mendenhall, where he sat in his study writing sermons, and tell him about his daughter's lapse from grace."[3] She also describes in detail the way in which she, then age four, got back at Norma Jean Bovey, a first-grader who was terrorizing her older sister:

> Now my sister had been told repeatedly that you must never hit someone smaller than yourself. This rule had been emphasized to protect *me,* but it lopped over onto Norma Jean, who was also smaller than my sister, and rules were rules, especially to my sister, who was very conscientious. What to do? Every day I sat on the porch

steps waiting for my sister to come home from school, and every day I saw her come weeping and pounding down the sidewalk with Norma Jean Bovey in hot pursuit. What to do indeed! Well, it all seemed pretty simple to me. Norma Jean Bovey may have been smaller than my sister, but she was *not* smaller than me. I took an Easter basket and filled it with rocks. ("Moral Dilemmas," 3)

In each of the anecdotes that Babbitt tells in "Moral Dilemmas and Doll Underwear" as well as in the autobiographical stories that are scattered through her published essays, it is clear that the events being recounted still have meaning for her, are still alive to her. In yet another story she recounts withholding, for several weeks, half the money she was supposed to put in the collection plate at Sunday school because she had made the pragmatic decision that Sunday school wasn't worth an entire ten cents. She was caught and punished, of course, but confides that "to this day I still mull over from time to time the problem of the ten pennies" ("Moral Dilemmas," 6).

The period from 1938 to 1944 was the longest that Babbitt had yet remained in one place, and she remembers those years with great affection. She writes, for example, of having had a "fifth grade of such perfection that the ages ten and eleven remain my favorite for my stories' young heroes and heroines" (autobiographical essay, 10). It was at this time, also, that Natalie, in a manner of speaking, made her first professional sales as an illustrator. Fascinated by the then popular Vargas girls, illustrations of long-legged, sexy young women, which rivaled Betty Grable in popularity as pinups in the Army barracks, she began drawing her own and selling them at school. "When my mother found out about it, she was scandalized and made me stop. I was ready to stop, anyway, because I couldn't at all match Vargas' rendering. I know why now: colored pencils simply couldn't do what an airbrush could do" (9). Babbitt claims to have been permanently influenced by her short career as a pinup artist. Even in college her art professors criticized her work for being too commercial.

For Natalie and her family, however, the moves from town to town were not over. In the spring of 1944, when Natalie was eleven and part way through sixth grade, her father took a job with the U.S. Department of Labor in Cleveland, and the family moved to suburban Willowick on the shores of Lake Erie. Unfortunately, the government position was short-lived and her father was soon out of work again. One positive side to the Cleveland move, from the point of view of Natalie and her sister at least, was the discovery that their school in Middletown had been far ahead of the Willowick school system and that they had essentially already mastered the curricula for their grades. Genevieve therefore had them excused from the last third of the school year, and they spent the spring and summer of 1944, as Babbitt puts it, "playing with Lake Erie" (autobiographical essay, 10).

If small lakes symbolize comfort and tranquillity in Babbitt's fiction, larger bodies of water symbolize mystery and potential danger. Babbitt writes in great detail about the effect that Lake Erie had on her: "The lake was a mysterious, exciting, living thing to me. . . . I think the weather in the region of the Great Lakes is more dramatic than anywhere else, including the seacoast. I have never seen, anywhere, anything to match Great Lakes blizzards and electrical storms. I loved them and I loved Lake Erie, too, and formed some deeply satisfying conclusions about the grand indifference of Nature to human life and endeavor—satisfying because I felt, and feel, that it is comforting to be reminded of our proper place in the scheme of things" (autobiographical essay, 10). Although Erie itself never plays a major role in Babbitt's fiction, she has used the feelings that the lake evoked in her, combining them with her later reaction to the Atlantic Ocean, in a number of her stories, particularly *Dick Foote and the Shark* and *The Eyes of the Amaryllis*.

In the fall of 1944 the Babbitt family moved again, to nearby Willoughby, Ohio, where Natalie began junior high school. In 1945, evicted by their landlady, they moved to Mentor, yet another Cleveland suburb, where they lived in a large farmhouse complete with a pond much like that in *Tuck Everlasting*. Although Ralph Moore had spent only a short time unemployed, the family was not by any means wealthy. Nonetheless, aided by partial scholarships, and much scrimping at home, they found the money to send first Diane and then, in the fall of 1947, Natalie to the Laurel School, a private and expensive girls' school where both Moore children received a superb high school education. Although Babbitt reports envying her wealthier classmates' after-school clothes, their convertibles, and their elegant homes, in general she was well accepted. Her sister Diane was an outstanding student and graduated cum laude before going on to Wellesley College. Natalie reports that she herself was an indifferent student, though good in English and art. Eventually, in the summer of 1948, evidently in order to be closer to Laurel, the family moved to the upper half of a duplex on the edge of Shaker Heights, at that time one of the most exclusive suburbs in the Midwest. Their house, Babbitt writes,"was a far cry from my friends' houses but my mother could turn any set of rooms into a little gem, so it was fine" (autobiographical essay, 12).

Natalie Babbitt's father emerges from her various autobiographical writings as a kind, witty, somewhat eccentric, but not very ambitious man who loved to play with words, pun, and tell amazing stories, He was particularly fond of making up crazy inventions like "a pep tonic for the elderly which he planned to call Cavort" (autobiographical essay, 4). He evidently hated affectation and had relatively little interest in getting ahead in life. Natalie's mother, Genevieve, however, was very much the opposite. Her father had died when she was small and her mother had never remarried, so she had grown up in a fairly poor home where women were expected to work. Her mother had supported them as a dressmaker. She was, moreover, proud of what she saw as her genteel ancestry, disappointed by her husband's inability to give her family the kind of life she wanted for them, aware of her own considerable talents, and, as Babbitt describes her, clearly, and quite rightly, a frustrated woman. Genevieve Moore apparently had a very real talent for art and achieved some success as a painter of portraits, landscapes, and still lifes. She also put herself through the Western College for Women, part of Miami University of Ohio, and, before meeting and marrying Ralph Moore, had saved enough money to take herself on a European tour. Unfortunately, while the family was living in Westerville, she was talked out of going to Ohio State University for a master's degree in fine art by the local church women who, as Babbitt relates the event, "paid her a visit and suggested that it was her place to stay at home with her children and stop all the career nonsense" (6). Worse still, her husband was totally unsympathetic and essentially refused to let her work as a teacher once they were married. (6).

Babbitt recounts that her mother, with no other outlet for her intelligence and energy, "turned the intense searchlight of her ambition on my sister and me" (autobiographical essay, 6). That this was an enormous advantage for Natalie is clear. She grew up assuming that she could do anything she wanted in terms of education and a career and still expect to have a happy marriage and a family. Her mother also saw to it that both of her daughters had all the advantages available. They went to the opera, symphony, art museum and theater whenever possible, took riding, art, and piano lessons, read widely, were enrolled in the Laurel School, and, under their mother's watchful eye (and their father's rather bemused and amused eye), made the right kind of friends (7).

Babbitt loved her mother and gives her much of the credit for her success. In her autobiographical writings she emphasizes the family's many good times: going on hikes, having wonderful parties, roller-skating and ice-skating, playing word games. All in all, she insists, it was "a supremely happy childhood, and quite normal, if not entirely average" (autobiographical essay, 8). That their mother's ambition had a negative side, however, is equally clear. As a child Babbitt seems to have found the constant push to succeed something of a drain. Although her "human skeleton" phase, coming as it did between the ages of six and twelve, occurred too early to be labeled true anorexia, such problems are often associated, even in young children, with family stress or performance anxiety. Genevieve died when Natalie was only twenty-four, and her daughter's ambivalence still runs deep. This shows particularly in the forbidding, snobbish, and tormented, but basically good character of Mrs. Goody in *Goody Hall,* whom

Babbitt has revealed to be a somewhat fictionalized version of Genevieve Moore. Winnie Foster's rather stuck-up parents in *Tuck Everlasting* may also owe something to Natalie's mother, as may the parents in Babbitt's early picture book, *Phoebe's Revolt.*

It seems to have been determined fairly early that Diane would be a writer when she grew up (she actually became a teacher) and that Natalie would be an artist, although as early as her junior year in high school she coauthored a musical comedy with a classmate. Her success as a playwright gave her mother the idea that Natalie should major in theater at college, so, in the fall of 1959, she entered Smith College in Northhampton, Massachusetts, intending to study set and costume design. Soon discovering, however, that a theater major would also require her to take acting and dance classes, two things she wasn't very good at, she quickly switched to a major in studio art. Babbitt writes that she and her mother began discussing the possibility that she would stay at Smith for two years and then return to the less expensive Cleveland School of Art for her degree. The cost of Smith was difficult to meet despite the fact that Natalie was working summers, primarily in the pricing department of a washing machine factory. Babbitt, although superficially happy, also felt an enormous social strain. Although she made friends, she was very conscious of both her relative poverty and her lack of social status. In the middle of her sophomore year, however, a friend set her up on a blind date with a junior from Yale named Sam Babbitt, and this changed everything.

Adulthood

As a contributing factor that led Natalie Babbitt to a successful career in writing and illustration, her mother stands out. Genevieve Moore gave her daughter the desire to succeed professionally and saw to it that she received the training needed to focus that desire and bring it to fulfillment. Her father, a useful counterweight to her mother, appears to have contributed a love of language, a whimsical sense of humor, and, perhaps most important, the ability to sit back and not take the world too seriously. Also of some importance, evidently, was her father's immediate family: "if anyone should ever care to know why I love fooling around with names and the language in general, the answer has to lie with that particular set of genes" (autobiographical essay, 3). Her Grandmother Moore's parents, hoping for a son and planning to name him after Robert E. Lee, weren't a bit fazed when they had a daughter; "they just shrugged and named her Roberta E. Lee. Roberta E. Lee Klotz" (3). She also remembers with fondness her Aunt Virginia, a one-time vaudeville actress who "got all the way to the Palace Theater in New York City with a baby act not too dissimilar from the one made famous by the great Fanny Brice" (3). Finally, Babbitt credits her Ohio upbringing with an enormous influence on her personality. In contrast with her mother's life-long, frustrated desire to be a New Englander, she has stated that "I myself am content to concede that my roots are all in Ohio" (2), and, talking about her lack of reserve, she has joked that "perhaps I should be reticent and aloof, but if you've got Ohio roots, that's hard."[4]

As an adult, however, Natalie Babbitt seems to have been influenced by three new and important factors: her husband, Samuel Fisher Babbitt; her discovery, through Betty Friedan's *The Feminine Mystique,* of the women's movement; and her relationship with Farrar, Straus, & Giroux editor Michael di Capua.

Babbitt has written that "if I had married another sort of man, I would probably—since I am fundamentally rather lazy—never have written a word."[5] She met Sam Babbitt on 2 February 1952. He was an "older" man (born 22 February 1929), the son of very wealthy parents (Babbitt refers to them as "genuine American aristocrats"), and a veteran who had returned to Yale after fighting in Korea. She records that:

> When I met him, he had been back from this nightmare
> only a few months, and had an attitude towards life quite
> different from that of other young men I knew. He was
> also blindingly handsome, he was wise, and scholarly,
> and, because he was a Whiffenpoof [a Yale man], daz-

zlingly glamorous. I made up my mind on the spot that wild horses and a room of my own at the Metropolitan Museum couldn't drag me off to the Cleveland School of Art. I stayed at Smith, learning absolutely nothing, and when I graduated in June of 1954, we were married and went to live in his home town, New Haven, Connecticut (autobiographical essay, 15).

They were married on 26 June 1954. Sam Babbitt had taken courses in creative writing at Yale, winning a major prize for his work, and had sold a story to *Collier's* magazine. Natalie therefore agreed to take a job while he stayed home and wrote a novel. She worked for several months in the Yale freshman dean's office, but by Christmas Sam realized that he didn't really like the enforced loneliness of the writer's life. She then quit her job—which she reports that she wasn't very good at anyway—and he took a position in the Yale administration. Although Sam Babbitt was later to go on to get a Ph.D. in American studies with a concentration in literature, he has spent virtually his entire professional life as an administrator, mostly with universities.

For several years Babbitt seems to have lived the typical life of a university spouse, making a home for her husband, accompanying him to university functions, raising children. Their first child, Christopher Converse, was born in 1956, and their second child, Thomas Collier, in 1958. Daughter Lucy Cullyford followed in 1960. Babbitt's husband, meanwhile, had taken a position as dean of men at Vanderbilt University, and the family had moved to Nashville in 1957. It appears to have been a lonely time for Natalie. Her mother had died the year before, and her father was in Thailand with the Labor Department. They knew practically no one at first, and she reports that "I always had a bucket of diapers in one hand in those days, and seemed to be slipping farther and farther away from that career as an illustrator I had wanted for so long" (autobiographical essay, 16). The situation did improve as she made new friends, and Babbitt grew to love her life in Nashville, but virtually her only creative work at that time was making posters for university activities. The highlight of her

years at Vanderbilt was a musical she and her husband collaborated on, which was performed by the faculty and administrators
to raise money for a faculty club.

In late 1961, swept up in the enthusiasm of the Kennedy era,
Sam Babbitt took the job of college and university liaison officer
for the Peace Corps, and the family moved to Washington, D.C.,
in January 1962. Babbitt records that it was the hardest move
that she ever had to make, a fairly strong statement considering
some of her childhood moving experiences. "Like my Grandmother Moore, I didn't want to go to Washington. I loved my life
in Nashville and dreaded being new again" (autobiographical essay, 17). Essentially she appears to have spent about eighteen
months being more or less miserable until, faced with the choice
between moving his entire family to the Philippines for a year or
two on Peace Corps business and returning to Yale for his doctorate, Sam chose the latter.

Her time in Washington, D.C., appears to have marked the low
point in Natalie Babbitt's adult life. Her husband and family gave
her enormous pleasure—indeed the strongest criticism she has
ever made of her husband in print is that he doesn't approve of
her taste in reading[6]—but, despite a happy family life, she
wanted something more. She was over thirty. Her career as an
illustrator appeared to be stillborn. Her husband stood as a daily
reminder that success was possible. She felt useless and frustrated. And then occurred what may have been the second major
event in her adult life. As Babbitt succinctly puts it, "Betty Friedan's *The Feminine Mystique* was published and it changed
everything once and for all" (autobiographical essay, 17).

The book, which she read some time in late 1964 or 1965, evidently had an enormous and immediate effect: "I can remember
perfectly a lunch I went to with my New Haven friends at which
we all yelled at each other, and banged on the table, and said
things we'd all been feeling for years but didn't know anyone else
was feeling, too. We talked—really talked—for the first time. As
a result, one left her husband, one went back to school, one threw
up her hands and had a fifth baby, and I—I said, 'By God, I'm
going to do what I've always wanted to ' " (autobiographical essay,

17). Her husband was studying for his Ph. D. oral exams at the time, but Babbitt, a woman possessed by an idea, was not to be denied. She had a title in mind for a children's picture book, *The Forty-ninth Magician,* and told her husband to write a story to go with it, which he did in two hours. Babbitt did a series of delightful pen-and-ink illustrations, and they sold the book to a young editor at Pantheon named Michael di Capua. When di Capua moved to Farrar, Straus & Giroux soon thereafter, Babbitt went with him. A mark of their mutual respect, di Capua still does Babbitt's books himself, though he is now editor in chief of Farrar, Straus & Giroux.

In 1966 Sam Babbitt became president of newly founded Kirkland College, a woman's school connected with Hamilton College, and the family moved to Clinton, New York. They bought a small house next to a pond in the foothills of the Adirondacks, a site Babbitt was later to use as the setting for *Tuck Everlasting.* They stayed in Clinton for twelve years, her longest single residence in one spot, and Babbitt remembers the period fondly.

Professionally these were very good years for Natalie Babbitt. Having gotten her feet wet as a professional illustrator, and with the encouragement of both her husband and di Capua, she began writing her own picture books. The first result, in 1967, was *Dick Foote and the Shark,* a Junior Literary Guild selection. It was followed in 1968 by another picture book, *Phoebe's Revolt,* and then, in 1969, by Babbitt's first full-length children's novel, the much-praised *The Search for Delicious,* which was chosen by the *New York Times* as the best novel of the year for nine- to twelve-year-olds and was a starred book on the American Library Association's annual list. During her years in Clinton she wrote or illustrated most of the books for which she is known today: *Kneeknock Rise* (1970), a Newbery Honor Book; *The Something* (1970), her last picture book until 1989; her almost Dickensian mystery novel *Goody Hall* (1971); *The Devil's Storybook* (1974), nominated for the National Book Award; and her two finest children's novels, *Tuck Everlasting* (1975), winner of the Christopher Award, and *The Eyes of the Amaryllis* (1977). It was the most productive period of her career.

Babbitt taught creative writing and illustration for children at Kirkland and made many valuable friendships, including one with the poet and novelist Valerie Worth, whose husband was a member of the Kirkland faculty. In 1972 they began an enduring collaboration when Babbitt illustrated Worth's first collection of poems for children, *Small Poems*. Their succeeding collaborations—*More Small Poems* (1976), *Still More Small Poems* (1978), the novel *Curlicues* (1980), and *Small Poems Again* (1986)—have received much praise.

In 1978, however, Kirkland College was absorbed by Hamilton, and Sam Babbitt was out of a job. Lucy, their youngest child, was beginning her freshman year at Smith College, and feeling the kind of freedom common to parents with a recently empty nest, the Babbitts decided to take an extended sabbatical on Cape Cod while Sam considered job possibilities. It was, evidently, a very good time for both of them. They had vacationed on the Cape in the past, but now fell in love with the area all over again. Babbitt worked in a tentative fashion on the manuscript of what would become her first adult novel, *Herbert Rowbarge*, but without much seriousness. She also accepted another major award, the George G. Stone Award for her work in children's literature. By the spring of 1979 Sam had decided to take a position as vice president for development at Memorial Sloan-Kettering Cancer Center in New York City. That spring the Babbitts also bought an old Cape Cod farmhouse in Dennis, Massachusetts, in which they currently vacation and to which they expect eventually to retire.

In September 1979 they moved into a rented high-rise apartment in New York City, and Babbitt, always a small-town girl at heart, was as unhappy there as she'd been in Washington, D.C., a decade or so earlier. Despite the museums, restaurants, theaters, and parks, the city, she writes, is "hideously expensive. To take advantage of what it has to offer requires a bankroll beyond the dreams even of my mother. And unless you go everywhere in a taxi, you have to have the legs of Atlas and a liking for powerful ocean winds blowing trash into your hair instead of leaves and milkweed" (autobiographical essay, 20). She enjoyed, in a bemused sort of way, the glittering, star-studded fund-raising efforts of the Cancer Center, which her husband, of course, was intimately involved in, and the job paid well, something the Babbitts, who had three children in college, very much appreciated. A high point of her New York years was her nomination, in 1981, for the important Hans Christian Andersen Medal. New York City was not conducive to writing, however, and it wasn't until 1982 that she was able to "wrestle *Herbert Rowbarge* into publishable form" (21).

In 1983 the Babbitts learned that Brown University in Providence, Rhode Island, was looking for a vice president for development. The money was somewhat less than Sam was making at Sloan-Kettering, but Tom and Lucy were now out of college and Chris was nearly through with graduate school, so money was a less crucial factor. Providence was only a couple of hours from Dennis, after all, and Brown University's educational philosophy was similar to that of Kirkland College. Sam applied for the job, got it, and by the summer of that year the Babbitts had left New York City, they hoped for good. They rented a home in Providence for one year then bought a small place of their own. Although she cannot help feeling a certain amount of skepticism, Babbitt cheerfully predicts that there will be only "one more move—when we retire to the Cape—but that will be that. I think. No more new houses, no more new places. Probably. So—moving van people, eat your hearts out. But I'm saving all the cartons and packing paper. No point tempting fate" (autobiographical essay, 21).

Since moving to Providence, Natalie Babbitt has produced two works, *Small Poems Again* (1986), her latest collaboration with Valerie Worth, and *The Devil's Other Storybook* (1987), a sequel to her National Book Award nominee of thirteen years earlier. She takes great pride in her children Christopher, a psychologist, Tom, a composer and rock musician, and Lucy, a children's novelist with two books of her own in print. Having just become a grandmother for the first time, she spends a portion of her time "knitting small things"[7] and, in a rather low-key, leisurely manner, is just beginning to consider ideas for another novel aimed at eight- to twelve-year-olds. She also does book reviews and occasional essays on various topics in children's literature. Although

Babbitt's books have never attained best-seller status, in the sense that the books of Judy Blume or Norma Klein have, her work can be clearly seen as both a critical and a popular success. In fact, with the exception of her first picture book, *Dick Foote and the Shark,* all of her published fiction remains in print. At fifty-five, Natalie Babbitt seems happy and content with her current life and, for the time being, relatively immobile.

2

Compromising with the Adult World
Dick Foote and the Shark
and *Phoebe's Revolt*

With her training in art, it was only natural that Natalie Babbitt should begin her career as an illustrator rather than as a writer. She did so in 1966 with *The Forty-ninth Magician,* written by Samuel Babbitt.

The story involves a boy king who promises his aging court magician that he will care for that gentleman's sons and grandsons for as long as they want to live in his castle. Unfortunately, as the years pass, things get out of hand because the magician has seven sons, each of whom has seven sons, all of whom are themselves magicians. Bored by their tricks and feeling crowded in his own home, the king decides to hold a contest to determine which of the forty-nine is the best. The winner will be named the King's Own Magician. The others will be asked to leave. In the hallowed tradition of such fairy tales, after forty-eight magicians have performed a series of spectacular magical feats, the forty-ninth and youngest wins the contest. He does this by taking the king out for a day in the country where they hike, create whistles by holding blades of grass between their fingers, build a waterwheel of reeds, and have a generally wonderful time. These simple pleasures make the hours go by like minutes, and this, the king decides, is the greatest magic trick of all.

Samuel Babbitt's story is spritely enough, combing good-natured humor with a worthwhile lesson in the value of simple pleasures, a theme Natalie Babbitt would herself use on several occasions. It is, however, her pen-and-ink illustrations that make the book. Babbitt combines a simple, cartoonlike line and strongly contrasting black and white areas, with a bewildering array of complexly textured medieval costumes to create dozens of clearly differentiated characters. Even in those illustrations that contain all forty-nine magicians, each comes across as an individual, and a humorous one at that.

Dick Foote and the Shark

Buoyed by the success of *The Forty-ninth Magician* and encouraged by both her husband and her editor Michael di Capua, Babbitt determined to write her own picture book. The result, *Dick Foote and the Shark,* a story in verse, appeared from Farrar, Straus and Giroux in 1967 and was immediately selected by the Junior Literary Guild.

Written primarily in quatrains of alternating anapestic tetrameter and trimeter lines, rhymed *a b c b, Dick Foote and the Shark* already demonstrates a number of motifs that would appear again and again in Babbitt's work. Like *The Eyes of the Amaryllis,* the book takes place on Cape Cod during the previous century, in 1873 in this case, and, as in that later novel, the ocean is an important element of the setting. As in most of Babbitt's books, the young protagonist does not fit within his environment and is missing a parent, in this case his mother, who is presumably dead. Dick Foote's father, John, a fisherman by trade, is a good man, but, like many of Babbitt's adults, is unable to appreciate his child's strengths. He considers the boy to be "lumpish and lack-brained and mulish"[1] and regards Dick's lack of interest in fishing as the great sadness of his life. Dick, however, is a talented poet, and his work is appreciated by other members of the community.

A theme at the heart of much of Natalie Babbitt's fiction is the need for the child to learn how to compromise with the adult world. For Babbitt, however, compromise is not so much a matter of selling out or of losing one's innocence as it is a way of growing, learning, and doing what is necessary to fit into society. Dick need not become a fisherman, he need not give up his dream of becoming a great writer, but he does need to achieve understanding and appreciation for what is not only his father's craft and the source of his own bread, but also the central fact of life on Cape Cod.

His fame as a poet having reached the city of New Bedford, Dick is commissioned to write verses for an upcoming town celebration, a poem "about fish, and the sea / And the fleet we are planning to bless" (*DF*, 8). The boy, however, knows nothing of the sea and, much against his will, must go fishing with his father to do the necessary research. At first he finds himself totally unable to appreciate the experience. He sits "sprawled very pale and appalled" (*DF*, 12), while John Foote sings and enjoys his work. Eventually, however, the boy begins to notice his father's obvious skills and to take mental note of the material he needs for his poem. Then, at day's end, a shark appears, a great brute with "a villainous grin" (*DF*, 16), intent on overturning the Footes' boat and eating both their catch and them. John Foote, knowing there is little hope, despairs of escaping the monster, but his son, unaware of the danger, is enormously excited and instantly composes a poem, "Oh, Glorious Queen of the Ocean!" in praise of the shark. The predator, "quite confounded with awe" at the boy's eloquence, pauses in its attack, and the Footes escape. As an outcome of their adventure, Dick, although he still has no desire to be a fisherman, learns to appreciate what his father does. Similarly, his father, although still wont to grumble, shows "a glimmer of pride that he couldn't quite hide" (*DF*, 26), when he thinks of his son's art. Perhaps more important from his point of view, he has gained a potent charm against sharks.

Throughout her fiction, Babbitt demonstrates an appreciation for both craftsmanship and hard work. Although seeing them as worthwhile in and of themselves, she also views these traits as indicative of their possessor's sense of self-respect. John Foote is not simply a fisherman; he is a skilled fisherman. He loves his work and takes pride in doing it well. Similarly, in *Kneeknock Rise*, Egan's Uncle Anson is a skilled clockmaker, and that skill is further reflected in his levelheaded attitude toward the world. In contrast, it is not the Tucks' poverty in *Tuck Everlasting* that demonstrates their tragic and eternal despair so much as it is their slovenliness, their inability or unwillingness to keep things up, to make repairs. In *Dick Foote and the Shark,* although Dick is by nature destined to be a poet and not a fisherman, it is important that he learn to value his father's work, that both Footes, father and son, realize that each is a skilled craftsman in his own way and that each is doing something that is worthy of the other's respect.

Natalie Babbitt's own growing craft as an artist is ably demonstrated in her illustrations for *Dick Foote and the Shark.* Strong lines and clearly defined areas of black and white again dominate her pictures, but she introduces both shading and colored washes in this book, and her figures are more realistic than they were in *The Forty-ninth Magician.* Babbitt's love for complex visual texture is still evident, but is less important here than is her use of historically accurate details in clothing, architecture, furniture, and ships' rigging.

Phoebe's Revolt

Babbitts' second solo picture book, *Phoebe's Revolt* (1968), written in iambic tetrameter couplets, is set in New York City in 1904. Phoebe Euphemia Brown is eight years old, younger than the adolescent Dick Foote, and her parents are decidedly well-to-do. She shares with Dick, however, the chosen role of outsider. Like him, she has interests that differ from those of her family and peer group. Phoebe is a tomboy. She hates "picnics, teas, parades"[2] and most of those other activities that the times sanctioned as proper for little girls of her social class, preferring to play with her kitten or chase a hoop in the park. Her revolt against the restrictions placed upon her by society, as exemplified by her parents and her nurse Miss Trout, takes the form of a refusal to wear the typically frilly little girl's clothes of the day. Although we are assured that Phoebe is generally a good child, she throws a series of tantrums in protest against the "hated bows / And dresses made of fluff and lace / with frills and ruffles every place." Instead, a George Sand in the making perhaps, she insists on wearing her father's clothes, "simple white and sober black / Unornamented front and back."

Phoebe's parents tend to discount her frustration until a particularly severe tantrum disrupts an expensive party they have thrown in her honor, and her father decides to take action. "You say you want to wear my clothes? / It *is* surprising, I suppose, / But still, I've got some things to spare / That I'd be more than glad to share." He then dresses his daughter in one of his shirts and a top hat and insists that she continue to wear his clothes for a week. The seven days over, Phoebe, although still angry, goes back to her own clothes without a word.

Phoebe's Revolt, however, is not a simple lesson in the use of ridicule as a child-rearing technique. Babbitt did not require Dick Foote to abandon poverty and become a fisherman; rather she set up a situation whereby the Footes could compromise, could each learn to appreciate the other's skill. Similarly, in *Phoebe's Revolt,* compromise is the final outcome. Phoebe's father, digging around in an old trunk, finds a picture of his wife at the age of eight, dressed in the fashion of 1880 and looking exceedingly glum. The portrait evidently spurs Mrs. Brown to remember her own childhood unhappiness with her clothes. She therefore has her seamstress create for Phoebe an entire new wardrobe of comfortable, more or less androgynous, but socially acceptable clothing, including "A simple sailor dress or two / In sober, modest navy blue." Taken with the idea, she even has similar dresses made for herself.

Phoebe, pleased with the freedom of her new clothes, wears them with delight and even agrees to dress "in ruffles, chin to hem," on those rare occasions when circumstances demand it. Like Dick Foote, she begins to understand that the attitudes and demands of the adult world are not entirely irrational and that compromise is often necessary. Like Dick, she finally realizes that there may be more than one legitimate side to a given issue. There may even be perfectly good reasons for a little girl of her time to dress in frills and lace on occasion. Also, like Dick Foote's father, Phoebe's parents gain a new respect for their daughter, coming to understand that she, too, is a human being with a right to opinions and preferences of her own. Their role as parents is, at least in part, to moderate those preferences. They must allow their daughter the freedom to grow in her own unique way, while neither limiting her unnecessarily nor giving her a total free rein, which she cannot yet handle.

Phoebe Brown's big city environment is much more complex than either the medieval world of *The Forty-ninth Magician* or the Cape Cod of *Dick Foote and the Shark,* and many of Babbitt's illustrations for *Phoebe's Revolt* reflect that complexity. She draws her characters with a softer, less regular line and with more varied shading than she had used in her previously published work. The visual texture of her characters' clothing, although less striking than in *The Forty-ninth Magician,* is often more subtle. Similarly, the sepia wash, which adds an antique, turn-of-the-century feel to *Phoebe's Revolt,* is used with much more sophistication than was the simple green wash of *Dick Foote and the Shark.* Further, a number of her backgrounds—a city street, a cathedral, an upper-class urban interior—are merely sketched, left half to the imagination, as if any attempt to draw them with a hard, clear line might overwhelm the characters in the foreground. Some backgrounds are omitted entirely, isolating and highlighting the characters, and especially close-ups of their facial expressions, on the page.

Babbitt still uses black and white contrasts to very good effect, stark black appearing in large areas exclusively in the clothes of Mr. Brown and a policeman. *Phoebe's Revolt* is not an explicitly feminist work, but it is clear that, in centering in on her father's clothes, what Phoebe primarily envies is his male prerogative of power, freedom, and action. She wants clothing that will free her for rigorous activity, and she connects that freedom with clothes that are "simple white and sober black." Unlike Babbitt's variously shaded female figures, who at times seem almost to fade into the sketched background, Mr. Brown, in his black coat, dominates every illustration in which he appears. Even in repose at

Illustration from *Phoebe's Revolt* by Natalie Babbitt. © 1968. *Reprinted by permission of Farrar, Straus & Giroux.*

the breakfast table or on a piano bench, his black-suited figure seems almost to jump off the page. In the book's final illustration, Phoebe, sporting a gap-toothed smile, stands at ease in her new sailor suit. It is not black—she has had to compromise—but it is very dark, presumably navy blue. Dressed in the darkest outfit worn by any female character in the book, she has clearly gained much of the freedom from restraint that she desired.

It seems clear that all three of Natalie Babbitt's early picture books share a common theme. Ultimately, all are concerned with the importance of the child's developing ego and individualism as demonstrated by his or her preference for one thing over another. The king in *The Forty-ninth Magician* discovers that he prefers the miracles of nature to those of magicians. Dick in *Dick Foote and the Shark* already knows that he prefers poetry to fishing, but must convince his father of the legitimacy of his preference. Phoebe prefers practical clothes to frippery, and she too must convince her parents that her preference is legitimate.

Traceable through the three picture books is Natalie Babbitt's own development as an illustrator. The cartoons that she created for *The Forty-ninth Magician* are great fun, but they lack the realism of her illustrations for *Dick Foote and the Shark*. That book, in turn, lacks the sophisticated use of shading, varied line, and wash to be found in *Phoebe's Revolt*. In *Phoebe's Revolt* Babbitt also begins to demonstrate a mastery of facial expression seen more fully in her later work as an illustrator in such books as *Goody Hall, The Devil's Storybook,* Valerie Worth's *Curliques,* and *The Devil's Other Storybook.*

In *Dick Foote and the Shark* and *Phoebe's Revolt* Babbitt also can clearly be seen to have grown as an author. *Dick Foote,* although a nice enough story, has obvious flaws. Babbitt's complex verse is cumbersome and, at times, distracting. This is especially true of the two extended examples provided of Dick's own poetry, which are neither particularly well written nor particularly well suited to the book's intended audience. The simple couplets of *Phoebe's Revolt* are less distracting and, for that matter, better verse. Furthermore, the situation in *Phoebe's Revolt* is a bit more morally complex than it is in *Dick Foote and the Shark*. Dick's realization that his father's work is valuable is, aside from a bout of seasickness, essentially painless. He does not have to give up anything to make his compromise. Nor does his father need to make any major changes in his life in order to begin to appreciate Dick's skills as a poet. Phoebe, on the other hand, does have to sacrifice to some extent. She is, for the most part, as Babbitt argues all children are, "powerless, innocent, . . . acted upon rather than acting."[3] By having Phoebe equate male clothing with freedom of action and by then placing her in a situation where she can only get part of what she wants, Babbitt demonstrates that personal freedom is in fact limited by what society views as acceptable, particularly for little girls. This theme will again be important in what is generally considered Babbitt's masterpiece, *Tuck Everlasting.*

3

The Child as Adult
The Search for Delicious and *Kneeknock Rise*

By the late 1960s, with three picture books in print, two of them entirely her own work, Natalie Babbitt was ready to tackle something more ambitious. Over the next seven years, the most productive period of her career as a writer, she published six books, four of them longer works clearly aimed at the older reading child. The first of these were the much praised *The Search for Delicious* (1969) and Babbitt's Newbery Honor Book *Kneeknock Rise* (1970). In these two books Babbitt again deals with the uneasy relationship between children and their elders, but the relationships she portrays are increasingly complex.

In Babbitt's earlier picture book, *Dick Foote and the Shark*, Dick wants to write poetry and is ridiculed by his father for refusing to enter the adult world as a fisherman. In *Phoebe's Revolt*, Phoebe's parents respond to her complaints about feminine clothing by forcing her to wear one of her father's shirts and a top hat. In each case Babbitt concentrated on the problems in relationships between parent and children and on the necessity for compromise. Although they are not perfect people, the parents in both picture books make decisions based on the real need to help their children make sensible adjustments to the restraints of society and convention, and the children have to learn to fit within the limits imposed by them. In return, however, the parents have to learn to respect their children's individuality and grant them the right, within limits, to be different. Dick's father may be a crusty old sea dog, incapable of appreciating art for its own sake, but he is also a poor man who has to make a living. He has a legitimate reason to object to Dick's spending his time on poetry. Phoebe's parents may be angered by her revolt, but they swiftly reach a logical compromise. The parents in both books come across as essentially sensible people.

In *The Search for Delicious* and *Kneeknock Rise,* however, Babbitt treats the adult-child relationship with a more obvious awareness of its ambiguities. In these two novels the adult world is again restrictive, forcing children to adopt acceptable and supposedly sensible modes of behavior. The adults in the two novels, however, are sometimes anything but sensible, and the restrictions they place on children, although not entirely wrong, are often capricious. Some of these adults seem so taken by their obsessions as to be only marginally competent to run their own affairs—let alone those of their children. By comparison to most of the adults they know, Gaylen and Egan, the twelve-year-old heroes of *The Search for Delicious* and *Kneeknock Rise,* respectively, although capable of both error and immaturity, are paragons of reason. They, in fact, come across as among the most serious and responsible characters in their books. Though both boys are rather naive and though both have something to learn about the meaning of life, neither acts primarily out of selfish or irrational motives. Though the adult world does finally exercise control over them, both boys prove themselves capable of making important decisions on their own.

The Search for Delicious

The Search for Delicious is set in a vaguely English never-never land referred to only as "the Kingdom" and tells the story of Gaylen's quest for the best possible definition of the word "delicious." His adoptive father, Prime Minister DeCree, is working on a dictionary and has chosen to define "delicious" as "fried fish," thereby provoking a near civil war when the King, the Queen, and the various cabinet ministers violently disagree. Meanwhile, Hemlock, the Queen's villainous and Machiavellian brother, lurks in the background, ready to take advantage of the deteriorating political situation and to stage a revolt. In an attempt to end the strife, the King sends Gaylen out to survey the Kingdom. The proper choice for the definition of the word "delicious" in DeCree's dictionary will, in effect, be decided by popular vote.

From the very beginning of her book, Babbitt shows us adults acting, not simply as children, but as very young children indeed. It is, of course, good dictionary practice to use examples to define abstract terms, but only a very young child or, perhaps, a person suffering from a severe right-brain dysfunction would conceivably confuse the term and its exemplum. Also, it should be noted that the question that Gaylen is sent out to survey the Kingdom on is not, "what is the most delicious food in the world?" but rather, "what is delicious?" Like a very small child, each adult character in the novel insists upon a concrete, one-to-one correspondence between the abstract term "delicious" and his or her real-world exemplum of that term. For the King delicious is apples. Period. There are no other possibilities, and anyone who thinks differently is obviously a fool. The Queen, equally adamant, insists on Christmas pudding, the General on beer, and so on.

It is, perhaps, appropriate that the hero sent on such a quest should be a twelve-year-old child. Gaylen performs his mission to the best of his ability, but it is clear from the beginning that, unlike the adults, he has no emotional commitment to finding an answer to the question. He alone, of all the people at court, remains uncommitted. He even confides to the Prime Minister that the thought of anyone starting a civil war over the definition of a word strikes him as silly. The boy adamantly refuses to express his choice for delicious, indeed appears not to have one, despite attempts by the King, the Queen, and the Prime Minister to influence him through bribery. For Gaylen, upon setting out at least, the quest itself is its own reward: "It all seemed very like a holiday and Gaylen, bouncing up and down on Marrow's broad back, was excited and happy. To ride out on a strong horse and to see the kingdom—this was very fine, indeed."[1] The boy will do his best to fulfill the King's command, but he honestly does not care about the answer.

To a certain extent Gaylen may be seen as a Candide figure, a wide-eyed innocent. Babbitt emphasizes the fact that, although he is an orphan, he has led a sheltered life and that if he "came to believe that the world was a bright and flawless garden where no weed grew ... it was not to be wondered at" (*SD*,18). The Prime Minister's decision to send Gaylen on the quest is thus based both on his belief that the boy is responsible enough to handle the job and on his feeling that Gaylen should "go about and see something of what the world is really like while you're still young enough not to get discouraged" (*SD*, 26–27). Gaylen, however, is not yet equipped to understand this remark. His naiveté makes it possible for him to begin his search without seriously reflecting upon either its purpose or its likelihood of success. He really knows nothing of the existence of any evil beyond the petty bickering of the court and thus has no reason to expect either that impediments might be placed in his way or that there might be someone who actively wishes him to fail.

Problems do, however, begin almost immediately. Only a few hours out from the castle, Gaylen, biting into an apple that the King had slipped into his saddlebag, hurts his teeth. Within the apple is a walnut, placed there by Hemlock, the Queen's brother. Nuts had been Hemlock's choice for "delicious" and his hiding of one within the apple might be seen as just another example of the court's bickering one-upmanship. The pain, however, is considerable, and Hemlock's maliciousness serves as Gaylen's first indication, the first of many, that real evil exists in the world.

Gaylen's discovery of evil is central to *The Search for Delicious*, though that evil is fairly simple and straightforward. It is clear throughout the novel that evil is essentially an outgrowth of selfishness and solipsism. It results from the individual's tendency to see things almost exclusively from his or her own point of view and from a refusal to grant others the right to their own viewpoint. The King and his court are unable even to consider the opinions of others. Even the Prime Minister, although he agrees with Gaylen that the controversy is silly, is still unwilling to give up his position in the matter. Hemlock, the villain of the book and a man of slightly more intellectual sophistication than the other adult characters, does not really care whether or not his choice, nuts, is picked as the definition of "delicious," but he is every bit as single-minded as anyone else in his pursuit of what he wants, control of the kingdom. He does not care who suffers as long as he gets his way.

Gaylen's entire quest, in fact, can be seen as a series of encounters with selfishness and solipsism. Each farmer, each townsman, sees Gaylen's request for "the food he or she honestly believes to be the most delicious of all foods" (*SD*, 29) as a direct threat to himself. Within days, sparked by the public's all too great willingness to believe Hemlock's claim that the King plans to ban some foods, a civil war breaks out, the two major factions defining themselves as Squashies and Crisps. Even the supernatural beings who live in the hidden and out-of-the-way parts of Gaylen's world—the dwarfs, the woldweller, the winds—refuse to become involved in any attempt to end the crisis. When Gaylen asks them for help, they merely respond, "It's nothing to us" (*SD*, 122).

To some extent the selfishness that Gaylen encounters may be seen as resulting from a failure of the imagination. The King, his courtiers, the various citizens of the Kingdom, all seem to spend most of their time obsessed with trivia. They are incapable of looking beyond the concrete facts of everyday life. They have even forgotten the ancient myths of their land or, if they remember the legends of dwarfs, woldwellers, mermaids, and such, see them as nothing more than delightful tales for children. Babbitt writes that "nobody believed they were real any more except for an occasional child or an even more occasional worker of evil, these being the only ones with imagination enough to admit the possibility of something even more amazing in the world than those commonplace marvels which it spreads so carelessly before us every day" (*SD*, 10).

It is, of course, traditional to see children as having more imagination and insight into what is important than adults and to see them as losing these things as they grow up—Wordsworth's "shades of the prison-house" closing in. Babbitt's equation of the adult imagination with evil, however, although a bit startling, also makes sense. "Workers of evil," like Hemlock, are presumably discontented with the world as it is. They thus have a tendency to use their imaginations more than other adults because they spend their time thinking in terms of alternate realities, realities where they can get what they want. Children, too, generally have good reason to be discontented with the world as it is because they have so little control over how the world affects them. For Babbitt, helplessness, the inability to control one's own life, is one of the central characteristics of childhood. In her essay "Who is 'The Child'?" she writes, "Let's face it: children are not a power group" (164). Young people hate feeling helpless, and, as anyone who has ever watched a ten-year-old boy kill monsters in his backyard can tell you, they frequently exercise their imaginations through fantasy and daydreaming to escape from those feelings. Babbitt suggests in another essay, "The Roots of Fantasy," that "fantasy is primarily a symbolic language for dealing with three very real and fundamental human attributes: we fear, we hope, and, because life can be very dull sometimes, we need to be diverted."[2] Children and malcontents, she seems to believe, because they spend more time fearing, hoping, and searching for diversion, share an openness to fantasy and the imagination.

And Gaylen's world, though most of the adults he meets may deny it, is full of fantastic beings. They are shy of humanity, for good reason, but "there are dwarfs in the mountains, woldwellers in the forests, mermaids in the lakes, and, of course, winds in the air" (SD, 5), each with its proper place, each responsible for taking care of its own particular environment. Gaylen meets a number of these beings in the course of his quest, but the mermaid, Ardis, is central to the story.

The Search for Delicious actually begins, not in Gaylen's day but centuries earlier, with what is essentially a creation myth. There was a time, Babbitt tells us, "long before there were any people about to dig parts of it up and cut parts of it off . . . and plague . . . each other with quarrels and supper parties" (SD, 5), when the Kingdom was a dry, dusty place, devoid of forests and much other life. Then, three dwarfs, digging in the mountains, accidentally discovered an underground spring, which eventually became the source of several rivers and made the land green. Over the spring the dwarfs built a small stone house with a rock door carefully balanced to open and close only at the sound of a magic whistle. Later, when the spring and stone house became submerged in a small lake, the dwarfs gave the whistle to the mermaid Ardis. She developed the habit of playing in the house each day with her doll, while leaving the whistle hanging from a rock on the lake shore. Unfortunately, she lost both whistle and doll when a wandering minstrel, finding the former, blew on it, unknowingly locking the doll within the stone house, as Ardis, hidden in the weeds by the shore, watched with horror. He then left, ignorant of what he had done, taking the whistle with him.

Gradually, people settled the Kingdom, and the various supernatural beings, angered by humanity's disrespect for the environment, withdrew into the mountains and forests. As the centuries passed, Ardis continued to live in her lake and continued to grieve for her lost doll.

The story of Ardis the mermaid is central to *The Search for Delicious* in several ways. First, Hemlock appears to be one of the few adults who has the imagination to believe in her existence, and he sees her as important. Although he tells Gaylen she is "only a dream" (*SD*, 53), it is clear that he has been searching for her for unsuccessfully for some time. On the most practical level, he is looking for her because he sees her as a possible source of interference with his plot to overthrow the King, which involves damming the river that flows out of her lake until the people, parched for water, capitulate. On a deeper level, however, Hemlock appears both wistful about never having found her and, at the same time, defiant. "What good are dreams, after all?" (*SD*, 53), he asks. Hemlock has imagination, but his imagination is limited by his need to evaluate everything in terms of its practical use. He is incapable of seeing the supernatural beings he has discovered, like the woldweller and the dwarfs, as marvels in their own right. Rather, he sees them merely as means to an end, as tools that will help him gain control of the Kingdom. Ardis, who

Babbitt draws and characterizes as a sort of eternal eight-year-old, personifies natural innocence and, because she is a child, a kind of uselessness. It is thus the height of irony that she and twelve-year-old Gaylen, rather than the King and the other adults, may well be responsible for the foiling of Hemlock's plot. Babbitt intentionally leaves Ardis's roll a bit unclear, however. Did the dam fail because a rock at its base was simply weak, as one of Hemlock's thugs suggest (*SD,* 134), or because Ardis undermined it at Gaylen's request? We never find out for certain.

Ardis and the other supernatural beings in *The Search for Delicious* also serve as vehicles for the development of one of Babbitt's most important reoccurring themes, the necessity for the individual to find a responsible place in society. Both Dick in *Dick Foote and the Shark* and Phoebe in *Phoebe's Revolt* had to demonstrate that their life choices, poetry and practical clothes, fit legitimately within the fabric of society, and Gaylen, too, must demonstrate that he can fill a responsible role. As an orphan he began life as an outsider, someone without ties or obligations. As assistant to and unofficial adopted son of Prime Minister DeCree he has led a good life and shown maturity far beyond his years, but he has never really been forced to commit himself to anything important. His willingness to do the poll is based primarily on a desire for adventure rather than on any loyalty to king or country. Only after discovering Hemlock's plot to overthrow the government does Gaylen find himself in a position that requires him to take responsibility and do something morally difficult.

At various points in the novel, as he begins to realize that Hemlock is up to no good, Gaylen requests aid from the woldweller, the dwarfs, and the winds, but they invariably refuse him. Each has his own insular purpose (taking care of the forest, taking care of the mountains, and so on), and each denies having any responsibility to aid humanity. Not even Ardis will help him until Gaylen, in effect, blackmails her by refusing to give her the whistle (which he had found earlier in the book) until she has promised to undermine Hemlock's dam. Gaylen himself comes very close to turning away from his own responsibilities. Angry at the silliness of the argument that engendered his quest, frustrated by the way it has been complicated by Hemlock's plots, disgusted by the refusal of others to help him, he seriously considers giving up: "'They've really begun the war,' he said to himself. 'And all over a word in a dictionary, the ninnies! . . . Where in the world do I belong?' he wondered again. 'Well, I don't belong down there,' he said out loud. 'Let Hemlock do what he wants. . . . It's nothing to me' " (*SD*, 126). Gaylen comes very close to abandoning his quest and going off to live with the dwarfs.

Ultimately, though, Gaylen (whose name, we have been told, means healer) realizes that he has to go on with his attempt to defeat Hemlock. As silly as the King, Prime Minister, and the other citizens of the Kingdom may be, they are still his people, and he has to help them. Further, there is the matter of love. Gaylen loves his adopted father, Prime Minister DeCree, and he is half in love with a little girl named Medley, the daughter of a town mayor who helped him on his quest. As personified by the dwarfs, woldweller, and other supernatural beings, nature can regard humanity from a distance and can remain uninvolved, but Gaylen cannot. He cannot say, with Ardis, "what has that to do with me?" (*SD*, 145), but must instead see himself as a member of society and take responsible action.

Fortunately for Gaylen, however, in becoming a responsible citizen, it is not absolutely necessary that he give up his imagination. Some compromise is possible. In an epilogue, set some thirteen years after Hemlock's defeat, we discover that Gaylen has grown up to be an important citizen of the Kingdom, has married Medley, has had a child, and, eventually, has become mayor himself. His marriage is a fortunate one because, as a little girl, Medley, too, met the woldweller and, as a adult, she, too, can still appreciate the wonders of the world. Now every April Gaylen and his family take a vacation from their responsibilities and go off to visit the woldweller in his forest, the dwarfs in their mountains, and Ardis, now happily reunited with her doll, in her lake.

The SEARCH for DELICIOUS

Natalie Babbitt

Cover illustration from *The Search for Delicious* by Natalie Babbitt. © 1969. *Reprinted by permission of Farrar, Straus & Giroux.*

And what does "delicious" turn out to be? What else but "a drink of cool water when you're very, very thirsty" (*SD*, 156).

Kneeknock Rise

Natalie Babbitt clearly finds it useful to isolate her young protagonists, cutting them off from the surety of parental authority, because she uses some variation on this plot device in virtually all of her novels. Gaylen is an orphan and, throughout most of *The Search for Delicious,* he is on his own, away from home for the first time. Willet in *Goody Hall* has lost his father and sees little of his possibly deranged mother. Winnie in *Tuck Everlasting* is kidnapped, Jenny in *The Eyes of the Amaryllis* is away from home visiting her grandmother. Like Gaylen, Herbert in *Herbert Rowbarge* is an orphan, and the book's other main characters, Herbert's daughters, have lost their mother. Egan, the twelve-year-old protagonist of *Kneeknock Rise* (1970), is also separated from his parents. On his own for the first time, he is visiting his aunt and uncle and attending the annual Instep town fair some forty miles from home.

Instep gained its name from its location at the foot of Kneeknock Rise in the misnamed and really not very imposing Mammoth Mountains. The fair is the big autumn event for the people living in the lands around Instep because it is their chance to hear the blood-freezing cries of the Megrimum, a terrifying if seldom-seen monster, which supposedly lives on the mist-covered top of Kneeknock Rise. Instep is a wealthy community, and its people, "made smug and rich by tourists and privilege,"[3] treasure the beast because it makes their town unique.

Egan gets on well with his Aunt Gertrude, his Uncle Anson, and their rather overweight dog, Annabelle, but he develops an immediate love-hate relationship with his annoying younger cousin Ada and her cat, Sweetheart. The Megrimum, however, quickly becomes the central focus of his stay at Instep. Virtually everything in the town, from souvenirs to gossip, revolves around the creature. Furthermore, another of Egan's uncles, Ott, a rather fey, poetic sort, has recently disappeared. Rumor has it that he may be the Megrimum's latest victim.

Egan, like Gaylen, in *The Search for Delicious,* is a serious straight-forward fellow, and his reaction to the creature at the top of Kneeknock Rise is immediate: he wants to find out what it is. Also like Gaylen, Egan finds himself surrounded by adults who seem highly ineffectual, on occasion almost half-witted. Aunt Gertrude is good-hearted but overly emotional and very superstitious. Uncle Ott, by reputation, is a virtual mooncalf. Uncle Anson, although more sensible, is fairly reserved and seems unwilling to commit himself to action. He appears content to sit back, smile at his wife's eccentricities, and devote his time to making clocks. In their personalities and relationship Anson and Gertrude seem almost to be a simplified version of Mr. and Mrs. Bennett in Austen's *Pride and Prejudice*—he the ironic, detached, and long-suffering husband, she the fond but foolish wife given to hysterics.

Belief and the evidence for belief are important issues in *The Search for Delicious.* Too often the adults who surround Gaylen seem to hold ferocious beliefs without adequate or, frequently, any evidence to support them. On the other hand, they also deny the existence of the very real supernatural beings who inhabit their world because those creatures are not immediately in evidence. Gaylen's superiority to the adults who surround him in *The Search for Delicious* is, at least in part, a function of his willingness to keep an open mind and to delay coming to conclusions about the nature of reality. In the case of the Megrimum in *Kneeknock Rise,* however, Egan is faced not with adult skepticism concerning the fantastic, but rather with unquestioning belief in it. The townspeople have no doubt that the monster exists. They have heard it on many occasions, after all, and a few claim to have caught glimpses of it, though no one has gotten a good enough look at the beast to provide a detailed description. Further, they are willing to believe and spread just about any story concerning the creature's supposedly bloodthirsty activities, because it is an enjoyable pastime and it is good for the tourism business. Egan, surrounded as he is by true believers, take the Megrimum's existence for granted, but, like Gaylen, he is impatient with beliefs founded on whimsy and a lack of specific information.

Although he is in general very level-headed and mature, Egan, like many children, especially those approaching adolescence, is both enormously curious about the world around him and extremely unsure of his ability to cope with that world. He hates having to comply with the seemingly ridiculous expectations imposed upon him by society, but, simultaneously, feels an almost obsessive need to live up to those expectations. He dreams off and on of climbing the Rise, discovering the truth about the Megrimum, possibly killing it, and thus gaining great fame and respect.

Eventually he does climb the Rise. Several things spur him on to do so. One is his discovery of his Uncle Ott's poetry. The verses echo and, perhaps, intensify Egan's own desire to have an adventure: "What's on the other side of the hill? / Hush, they told me. No one knows. / I'll climb and see for myself! I will!" The boy, however, fails to understand the irony that often underlies Ott's verses: "I'll climb, I said, and see. I will! / Here's what I saw when I reached the top: / Another hill" (*KR,* 44). Egan does, however, appreciate Ott's own intense dislike for societal expectations:

> Annabelle eats without a spoon.
>   Nobody scolds if she sleeps till noon.
> And Annabelle strolls in the marketplace.
>   With nothing on but her awkward grace.
> But I wear hats and must live with hope,
>   And polish my face with terrible soap
> And hide my verses and show my smiles
>   And listen to everyone else's trials.
> Annabelle's lucky. Annabelle's free. (*KR,* 47)

Yet another of Ott's poems sets up a dichotomy very much like that which Gaylen must come to terms with in *The Search for*

Delicious between social responsibility and the happiness that comes from having an imagination:

> The king was gray with wisdom got
> From forty years of school.
> The Fool was pink with nonsense
> And could barely write his name
>
> . . . .
> The fool was gay. The king was not.
> Now tell me if you can:
> Which was perhaps the greater fool
> And which the wiser man? (*KR*, 48)

Reading these lines, Egan ponders over whether their author would have had to have been more like the king in the poem or the fool, and he wonders if it might be possible to "be gay and wise both at the same time" (*KR*, 48). This, in a nutshell, is the lesson he himself has to learn. His Aunt Gertrude has considerable imagination and takes great pleasure from life, but she has no wisdom to keep her fancy in check. Egan, on the other hand, has considerable wisdom for his age, but, like many unsure children, tends to take things too seriously.

The boy's overseriousness is well demonstrated by his vulnerability to the taunts of his younger cousin, Ada. Too often with children, what is said hurts regardless of whether or not it has any truth to it, and Ada's insistence that Egan is afraid to climb Kneeknock Rise, although not really true, is the final spur to the boy's desire.

Egan's climb, accompanied only by the dog Annabelle, is an exciting adventure, but ends in anticlimax when the monster he hopes to slay turns out to have no more substance to it than the heavy mist that enfolds the top of Kneeknock Rise. Rather than the Megrimum, he discovers his Uncle Ott who, rather than having been eaten, has simply been camping out. Ott tells Egan that "There isn't any Megrimum. Never was. It's all been just . . . a lot of—megrimummery" (*KR*, 83). What Ott has found instead is a hot mineral spring: "The water boils up to the top through a narrow hole .. and that makes this steamy mist . . . and the steam makes the whistling, whining, moaning sound" (*KR,* 84) of the Megrimum.

Egan had hoped to kill the monster and now realizes that, in a way, he can do just that be denouncing the fraud and making people aware that there is indeed nothing to fear. To his surprise and anger, however, no one is interested in having the Megrimum's legend debunked. The people of Instep ignore his claims or assume that he is feverish and insist that Annabelle, who actually went away with Uncle Ott, must have been eaten. Most of them are quite sincere in their refusal to believe Egan, and it is not simply a matter of preserving the tourist trade. When Egan asks his uncle if he thinks the Megrimum is real, Anson replies, "I think it doesn't really matter. The only thing that matters is whether you want to believe he's there or not. And if your mind is made up, all the facts in the world won't make the slightest difference" (*KR,* 111). Uncle Anson's point is that the Megrimum, whether real or not, serves several useful purposes. The monster makes money for Instep but, more important, it gives the people something to be proud of, something to feel special about, something to obscure the fact of their otherwise totally mundane existence. As Babbitt writes in an epigram at the beginning of *Kneeknock Rise,* "Facts are the barren branches on which we hang the dear, obscuring foliage of our dreams" (*KR,* viii). It may be foolish to believe in something that is not there, but we all need to be a little foolish now and then. We need to stretch our imaginations, to feel the joy that comes from confronting the unlikely and the amazing. At one point Uncle Ott asks Egan, "Is it better to be wise if it makes you solemn and practical, or is it better to be foolish so you can go on enjoying yourself?" (*KR,* 87), and it seems clear that Anson and Babbitt, at least in part, agree with this latter sentiment.

Much of the best literature for children and adolescents is, at its heart, largely about the child's gradually developing ability to see through illusions. For Natalie Babbitt, the truth rarely exists as a simple, easily grasped idea. Furthermore, the whole truth is not always what is wanted. Sometimes people are better off with parts of the truth or with a compromise between conflicting truths. Gradually Egan reaches a compromise between his own beliefs and those of Instep by coming to terms with the Megrimum's subjective reality. He still recognizes that hard facts and the literal truth are important, but he has discovered that there are also spiritual truths, imaginative truths. In *The Search for Delicious* the dwarfs and mermaids turn out to be real. In *Kneeknock Rise* the Megrimum turns out to be fantasy. Yet, as Egan's Uncle Anson implies, for those who believe in them, the actual existence or nonexistence of these beings is less important that the feelings that they invoke. Ultimately it is the imagination, with all of its fantasy and foolishness, that provides the joy that makes life worth living. Gaylen, in *The Search for Delicious,* grows up to hold a responsible position in the adult world as mayor, but he still manages to keep his imagination alive with a yearly visit to the dwarfs, the woldweller, and Ardis the mermaid. What Egan had first found annoying about Uncle Anson in *Kneeknock Rise*—his unwillingness to take a stand on the question of the Megrimum's existence—is eventually revealed to be not passivity or foolishness but rather Anson's own understanding that the people of Instep need the Megrimum and are not harmed by it. After all, as Geraldine De Luca has pointed out, "what the Megrimum does is give shape and meaning to the lives of people who would lead simple existences in any event."[4]

Egan, too, must learn to balance the serious and rational side of his nature with the imaginative side. Rationality without imagination leads to a boring, mundane existence and an obsession with the meaningless details of life. Imagination without rational control leads to superstition and solipsism. By realizing that other people need the Megrimum and by learning to accept that the creature does exist in a peculiar sort of way, Egan demonstrates flexibility, imagination, and a concern for others. By the end of *Kneeknock Rise,* he, like Gaylen in *The Search for Delicious,* achieves a healthy compromise between the practical and the imaginative, which brings him to a maturity few of the adults in his world can match.

4

Childhood Fears
The Something and *Goody Hall*

What do children fear the most? Things that go bump in the night? The ridicule of their peers? The loss of a parent? The seemingly insurmountable responsibilities that come with growing up? The writers who have best dealt with such childhood terrors, from Charles Dickens and Charlotte Brontë to Ray Bradbury and Ursula K. Le Guin, have generally been able to do so because they are more closely in touch than are most adults with what terrified them as children, and this seems to be the case with Natalie Babbitt. Although she has never written an openly autobiographical novel, many of her books clearly deal with insecurities traceable to her own background, whether it be fear of moving to a new home or anxiety about living up to the expectations of an unusually demanding parent.

Throughout her career Babbitt has demonstrated a clear sense both of the insecurities involved in being a child and of how those insecurities continue to affect us as adults. Many of her books center on a character's need to confront his or her fears and, when detailing such confrontations, Babbitt invariably avoids both oversimplification and condescension. In *The Search for Delicious* the crisis of confidence that almost causes Gaylen to abandon his quest is triggered, in part, by his alienation from the adult world, by his fear that he can never fit in. Egan's decision to track down the Megrimum in *Kneeknock Rise* is forced upon him, to some extent, by his cousin Ada's taunts. Better to face a monster than to have another child brand you a coward. In Babbitt's next two works, the picture book *The Something* (1970) and her gothic novel *Goody Hall* (1971), several of the most common childhood fears are of central importance.

The Something

The illustration technique of *The Something* differs considerably from that of Babbitt's earlier picture books. Absent are both the hard lines of *The Forty-ninth Magician* and the realism of *Phoebe's Revolt*. Opting for what are clearly cartoon characters rather than real people, Babbitt fills her page with hundreds of tiny pen strokes, which provide both detail and shading. The backgrounds and the shading, in fact, seem closer to the work of Edward Gorey than to anything in Babbitt's previously published work. Babbitt also abandons the wash technique that she used in *Dick Foote* and *Phoebe's Revolt,* replacing it with a subtle use of colored paper. Most of the book's illustrations are rendered using black ink on a white background and, with their considerable shading, are fairly dark, as befits the story of a child troubled by night fears. Babbitt decreases the effect of this darkness on the reader, however, by surrounding each illustration with a thick border of friendly pale yellow. Then, for a key dream sequence in which Mylo, the book's protagonist, must confront his fears, she replaces both the white background and the yellow border with a uniform, forbidding gray. Finally, when Mylo awakens, having been successful in his confrontation with the unknown, Babbitt ends her picture book with a return to white backgrounds and yellow borders.

Mylo is an endearing but ugly troll child. With his fur-covered body and long, skinny arms and legs, he seems vaguely reminiscent of Cousin It from the Addams Family. Mylo's chin and forehead both recede drastically. He has buck teeth and a wart on his nose. He lives in a cave. For all this, however, he is still a child. He loves his mother—a taller, but equally ugly version of himself in slippers, curlers, and housedress—and he spends much of his day in pursuits that seem more or less typical for a child—playing with clay, reading an ABC book, combing his arm fur.

Mylo, like many children, is "very much afraid of the dark,"[1] though, as is often the case, he has trouble articulating his fear. It is not ghosts or robbers that scare him, but "a Something" that might come for him at night through the hole in the cave wall that serves as his bedroom window. His mother buys him some modeling clay, hoping to take his mind off his night fears, but Mylo uses the clay constructively to come to terms with what is bothering him. He attempts to objectify his fear by making a clay statue of it. Eventually he finds himself "almost wishing it *would* come in through the window, so he could get a good look at it and make a better statue in the morning."

Having put a face to his fear, Mylo is ready to confront it. It is at this point, when the troll child falls asleep and begins to dream, that Babbitt makes the switch from white, yellow-bordered paper to dark gray paper. In his dream Mylo wanders "out in the wild dark," a maze of dimly seen, intertwining tree branches, until he sees the Something climbing through a windowlike hole in the maze. From Babbitt's illustrations it is immediately apparent that the Something is hardly the frightful monster Mylo feared. Rather, in a delightful role reversal, it is a barefoot little girl in a nightdress who, it turns out, is also asleep. Although there is a brief confusion over who has proprietary rights to their shared dream, the children quickly agree that they are not afraid of each other and that each is actually rather glad to have met the other.

Having conquered his fear, Mylo has no more use for the clay his mother bought him. He is ready now for more mature activities, and, as *The Something* nears its end, he settles down with his ABC book to read. The statue, however, he keeps as a memento.

Many children suffer from night fears—the thing under the bed, the thing in the closet. Many adults, although unwilling to

admit it, suffer from equally irrational, if somewhat more complex, terrors, both asleep and awake. Babbitt's lesson, therefore,
if a bit obvious, is one that is worth restating. Fears left uncon-
fronted are the worst. Put a name and a face to that which terrifies you, deal with it creatively, and, suddenly, you are back in
control. It has even been suggested by Anita Moss that Mylo actually needs the Something, finding a "piquant pleasure"[2] in his
terror, or at least in confronting it. Her point seems entirely in
line with the need mentioned earlier of the villagers of Instep for
the Megrimum in *Kneeknock Rise*. This possibility is underlined
by Babbitt's appealing use of role reversal, a plot device exactly
calculated to encourage children to see their night fears in a new
and unintimidating way. If you are afraid of monsters when *you*
go to bed, what do you think the monsters are afraid of when *they*
go to bed? The revelation that anxious troll children sometimes
dream of little girls is likely to surprise and delight any small
child, and the assurance that those dreams need not be frightening is likely to be a comfort. Babbitt's picture book, like many
of the best children's books, is thus about passages. Mylo's Something stands for all those unknown things that children find
frightening. By coming to terms with the thing he fears, by realizing that it is nothing more than a little girl, Mylo gains competence in dealing with the world. Presumably he will go on to
generalize that competence to include other unknowns, other
Somethings, as he continues to progress toward adulthood.

Goody Hall

When Franklin Roosevelt proclaimed in his first inaugural ad-
dress that "the only thing we have to fear is fear itself," he was
drastically oversimplifying the problems facing our nation, but
the implications of his statement were valid nonetheless. Fear
paralyzes our ability to evaluate and deal with a situation and
thus, in and of itself, becomes a cause for increased anxiety. Fear,
divorced in our minds from the events that stimulated it, can fre-

Illustration from *The Something* by Natalie Babbitt. © 1970. *Reprinted by permission of Farrar, Straus & Giroux.*

quently both obscure those events and make them seem more dire than they are. Natalie Babbitt is intensely aware of this fact. For many of her characters, the most frightening and difficult thing of all is facing up to what terrifies them. Again and again in her books, characters who have felt great fear and run from it eventually discover that, when they stare their fear in the face, it becomes less terrifying and more manageable. Gaylen's temporary abandonment of his quest in *The Search for Delicious* is, in large part, an attempt to avoid the rejection that he fears awaits him. Upon facing what he is afraid of and realizing that he cannot sever his link with the rest of humanity, he finds the strength to carry on. In *Kneeknock Rise*, the Megrimum is deliciously terrifying only so long as it remains a mystery. Mylo is afraid of the Something only because he does not know what it is. Upon giving it form, first in clay and eventually in his dreams, he discovers that there is nothing to fear.

Goody Hall is a story full of characters who cannot face up to their fears and who have kept secrets that they should have shared long ago. It is also a tale of misplaced persons—long-lost fathers who may or may not be dead, mothers who place impossible expectations upon themselves and their children, and sons who can not be what their mothers want them to be. Each character in the novel is an actor of sorts, playing a role designed to fit the expectations of others, without regard to whether or not that role allows for happiness. Because Natalie Babbitt believes firmly in the importance of happy endings,[3] however, all of the major characters will eventually learn to face their fears and will thus come to terms with who they really are.

What do children fear most? According to a recent study, more than anything else children around the world are terrified of the loss of a parent.[4] No other anxiety looms larger in the minds of the young. Several years previous to the beginning of the novel, young Willet, the heir to Goody Hall, has lost his father, supposedly in a riding accident, and this event is still the central circumstance of the boy's life. Further, Willet is obsessed with the belief so common among young children who lose a parent that his father is still alive. Such beliefs, of course, are usually nothing more than wish fulfillment fantasies, but, Willet has evidence. First, his mother, he says, never grieved for her husband's death, showing instead merely anger and frustration. Second, when they carried the coffin down the steps into Midas Goody's tomb, Willet "was hiding [nearby]. . . . They thought I was in the house, but I was really in the hedge. The coffin bumped against the wall and something inside it went *clank*."[5] Dead bodies, as the boy points out, do not clank. Something other than his father must have been in the coffin.

Since his father's supposed death, Willet Goody and his mother have lived a stagnant, isolated existence in their great "wedding cake" (*GH*, 10) of a house, seeing almost no one but their servants, their routine broken only by Mrs. Goody's periodic and mysterious trips to London. Willet's mother seems enormously depressed and brittle. Although it is apparent that she is obsessed with the beauty and ostentation of luxurious Goody Hall, it is equally obvious that the place makes her intensely uncomfortable and that she is out of place there, like "a slice of bread" in "a jewel box" (*GH*, 17). It seems clear that her heart is burdened by secrets that she cannot share with her son. Willet, in turn, loves his mother, but finds her enormously difficult to deal with because she expects things from him that are inappropriate for his age and wants things for him that he simply does not understand. Depressed and alone, not allowed to play with the boys from the nearby village, Willet spends most of his time either sulking or causing trouble for the servants.

Everything changes, however, when Hercules Feltwright, a wandering and not very competent actor, is hired to be Willet's tutor. Hercules, too, has had problems with parental expectations. These problems began at birth when his mother, deciding that her son was born to be a hero, both burdened him with a hero's name and began interpreting everything he did as if each act were one of the labors of Hercules. Thus, when as a baby, he accidentally rolled over on an earthworm that a neighbor boy had put in his cradle, his mother equated this with the baby Hercules' strangling of a poisonous snake with his bare hands. Similarly, when, as a child, he killed a cat that had run mad, she insisted that this feat was somehow the equal of the ancient Hercules' slaying of the Nemean Lion. In jarring contrast to his mother, Hercules' father, a hat maker, was a prosaic sort and wanted nothing more than for his son to join him in his trade. Unfortunately, Hercules Feltwright could not be happy as either hatter or hero and, wanting only to be "his own true self" (*GH*, 23), ran away and became an actor. On the stage, he thought, "I can try on as many different selves as possible and choose the one that seems to be the best and most comfortable fit"(*GH*, 27).

Willet and Hercules like each other immediately, and the tutor swiftly agrees to help the boy get to the bottom of the mystery. The plot of *Goody Hall* is complex, and many questions need to be answered. If Midas Goody is, in fact, alive, why did he choose to disappear? Whose body was it that was brought in from the road after the supposed accident? What object now resides within the coffin? Why does Mrs. Goody make her secretive trips to London, and how did the bishop's jewels get hidden in her hassock? How much does the gypsy clairvoyant Alfreida Rom actually know? Who exactly is the mysterious character seen lurking about Goody Hall late at night, and how is one to explain his uncanny resemblance to the legendary thief Mott Snave?

Eventually, Willet and Hercules clear up all of these mysteries, and when they do it becomes apparent that Babbitt has designed everything to reinforce her central theme. Most of the major characters in *Goody Hall,* we realize, have suffered in large part because fear has made it impossible for them to face important truths and has caused them to pretend to be something other than themselves. Midas Goody's actual name, we discover, is John Constant, and he was originally a farmer. Dissatisfied with his life, he developed an alter ego, the thief Mott Snave,[6] and began to steal things under that persona, only to return them under his own name, thereby gaining fame as a do-gooder. Then, when the local bishop bragged about owning a silver statue of the three-headed dog Cerberus and dared people to steal it, Constant, as Mott Snave, did just that. He had planned to return the statue, but, unfortunately, the bishop fell down a well while chasing him and drowned. With no one to return the statue to, or the jewels hidden inside it, the Constants kept them, moved a hundred miles south, changed their name to Goody, and built palatial Goody Hall.

Both were actually unhappy in their new surroundings, though Mrs. Goody convinced herself that she loved the house. Goody Hall, which came to symbolize for her the very notion of the good life, seemed to take on a personality of its own, virtually forcing its standards on those who inhabited it. Hercules notices this almost immediately, commenting that "If this house had its way . . . it would make me over into a regular dandy." He feels as if the parlor "in which he sat . . . pressed on him" and "insisted" that he behave properly (*GH*, 93). He realizes that Goody Hall, somehow, is to blame for Willet's problems, "but the house was to proud— and too beautiful—to care" (*GH*, 69). For Mrs. Goody, however, deluded by its elegance, the Hall became a symbol of everything worthwhile, of everything she wanted for young Willet, and she almost never left the building. Her husband, however, grew to hate Goody Hall, realizing that it simply was not in his nature to live an idle and pretentious upper-class life. He tried half-heartedly to convince his wife to leave but, failing in this, determined to escape. Faking his own death, he disappeared. Later he confessed to his involvement in the bishop's death and served five years in prison.

Because he could not be satisfied with who he was, Midas Goody nearly destroyed his family, ended up in jail, and spent ten years away from the one thing he really loved, farming. Because she forced herself to ignore who she was, Willet's mother made herself, her husband, and her son miserable. Farming had also been her life, but she forced herself to give it up, along with the dog, the garden, and the hard work she had enjoyed as a girl, in exchange for empty, meaningless wealth. Even young Willet must bear some of the blame. Because he does not want to disappoint his mother, he suffers in silence, glumly accepting her social pretentions, pretending that he loves life at Goody Hall. All three, in effect, live a lie, whether it be a lie of commission or omission. As Hercules says to Willet, "You tell me how she's been fooling you, about your father and all, but don't you see, Willet—you've been

fooling her, too. Everybody's been fooling everybody all along.
Maybe it's time to stop doing that. Maybe you should . . . tell her
right out how you really feel. Maybe she's unhappy, too" (*GH*,
137–38). When Willet reveals his true feelings to his mother, she,
after a moment's consternation, realizes that she also has been
miserable. Her husband, it turns out, has been released from jail
and, dressed as Mott Snave, has been lurking in the neighbor-
hood, hoping to convince his wife to return to their old farm. The
story ends happily when the Goody family does just that, after
first burning down cold, ostentatious Goody Hall.

Despite its complex plot, *Goody Hall* can be seen on a thematic
level as a fairly straightforward morality tale, at least so far as
the fate of the Goody family is concerned. Hiding from the truth,
pretending to be someone other than who you really are, causes
pain. Honesty, particularly to oneself, is the best policy. The character of Hercules Feltwright, however, is another matter. Like the
Goody's, Hercules is in large measure on the run from his past.
Like them, he originally left home because he was dissatisfied
with the role laid out for him there. Like them, he decides by the
end of the novel to return home and confront that past. Unlike
the Goodys, however, who were apparently dissatisfied with their
lives for no very good reason and who in fact do seem best-suited
to be farmers, Hercules had a legitimate reason to leave home.
Although he was good at hat making, his whimsical and impractical temperament made him unsuited for life as a tradesman
and, after all, no mere human being could conceivably have lived
up to his mother's heroic expectations.

Furthermore, it is clear that Hercules' absence from home has
caused him very little pain. When we first meet him on the road
he seems totally carefree: "He had been singing all the way from
the village, swinging the scuffed old satchel from one hand and
gesturing with the other from time to time when he felt the song
required it, and his long face was blissful and absorbed" (*GH*, 10).
Despite his enthusiasm, we can assume that Hercules Feltwright
is probably a fairly poor actor. His hilarious accidental travesties
of Shakespearean verse, evidence of all the lines he must have
blown on the stage, point to a decided lack of talent. Yet there is

no indication that his shortcomings as an actor have scarred him in any significant way. His decision to leave the stage and become a teacher, for example, resulted not from an awareness of failure as an actor but, rather, because he fell in love with the idea of teaching after playing the role of a schoolmaster. Nor is his decision to return home arrived at with any great difficulty. Rather, it comes to him easily and spontaneously: "embarrassed but pleased" by the "borrowed joy" of the Goody family reunion, Hercules, "all at once, with all his soul . . . longed for a reunion of his own. The charms of [his home town], so long neglected, rose up in his memory like a siren's song, sweet and irresistible" (*GH*, 161–62). Furthermore, he knows exactly what he is going to do when he gets there—open a school. Babbitt, as always, denies the simple answer. The Goodys were wrong to run away from their origins, but this isn't invariably the case. Hercules had to leave home, had "to try on as many different selves as possible" (27), in order to find his proper place. His dissatisfaction, unlike the Goodys', was legitimate.

Goody Hall, despite its many excellent features and its critical success, is actually one of Natalie Babbitt's less popular books. Perhaps this is a function of the complex plot, perhaps a result of her readers' uneasiness with the very real suffering of the Goody family. The light hand with which the delightful and memorable character of Hercules Feltwright is drawn may come from Babbitt's realization that her novel does have a fair amount of darkness in it. No character in *The Search for Delicious, Kneeknock Rise,* or the three picture books, after all, ever goes through the kind of pain that Willet's mother inflicts upon herself.

Although she is a secondary character in the novel, Mrs. Goody is of particular interest to students of Babbitt's life and fiction. She bears a distinct similarity to the author's own mother, Genevieve Converse Moore, a woman of middle-class background who, like Mrs. Goody, was very nearly obsessed with achieving upper-class status and providing the best of everything for her children. More important, however, she serves as a kind of warmup exercise for a number of major characters in Babbitt's later fiction. Mrs. Goody cannot come to terms with her past. Although there is nothing in it to be ashamed of, she has turned her lower-class background into a veritable skeleton to be hidden in the closet. Hardly rational on the subject of her childhood, she is fully capable of rhapsodizing over the joys of gardening or listening to her father play the fiddle in one breath and then, stopping herself in mid-sentence, of denigrating the life that gave her these things in the next. She sees her past as an inescapable and degrading memory, something forever to be dragged behind her, like Marley's chains in *A Christmas Carol*. Only after realizing that she has no need to escape from her past, and indeed no longer wants to, can she be happy. A similar inability to come to terms with the memory of past experiences is central to the problems of Geneva Reade in *The Eyes of the Amaryllis,* the Tuck family in *Tuck Everlasting,* and the title character of *Herbert Rowbarge.*

For Natalie Babbitt the past often holds the key to the future. That which we feared as children can continue to haunt us and limit us as adults, and only by recognizing what we are afraid of can we become whole people. At the end of *Goody Hall,* when asked where the Goodys have gone, the gypsy answers, "They went back. . . . *And* on. To better things" (*GH,* 176). By realizing both what their mistakes were and why they made them, Mr. and Mrs. Goody gain valuable insight into their own lives. By returning to the farm they should never have left, the Goodys both regain their rightful place in society and resume life as a family.

5

The Devil as Sad Sack
The Devil's Storybook and
The Devil's Other Storybook

Natalie Babbitt's spritely and ironic *The Devil's Storybook* (1974) and its sequel *The Devil's Other Storybook* (1987) fall neatly into that long tradition of literary works that use the character of Satan to demonstrate and make fun of humanity's moral failings. Her satire, however, as befits a work for children, is less sharp than that of other authors such as Ambrose Bierce in *The Devil's Dictionary* or, for that matter, John Updike in *The Witches of Eastwick*. Babbitt introduces her first collection of short stories with a quote from "The Devil's Walk" by the British romantic poet Robert Southey (1774–1843):

> From his brimstone bed, at break of day,
> A-walking the Devil is gone,
> To look at his little snug farm of the World,
> And see how his stock went on.[1]

These lines, with their oblique reference to the Book of Job, accurately convey the tone and content of both *The Devil's Storybook* and its sequel. The two collections, each containing ten humorous quasi folktales—some parablelike, many with a slightly Eastern European flavor—describe the adventures of a devil much closer to Til Eulenspiegel or Beetle Bailey than Milton's Satan. The

Devil, whom Babbitt portrays as slightly foppish and potbellied, and given to writing poetry, walks the earth playing practical jokes on farmers and their wives, beautiful women and young gallants, priests, and merchants. Unfortunately for him, he is not very smart, and his pranks, as often as not, backfire. Minor unhappinesses occur, but in general, those who suffer at the Devil's hands clearly deserve it. In the manner of such folktales, the truly good are invariably preserved by their goodness, and a clever farmer is more than competent to make a fool out of the Devil.

Babbitt's Hell is a relatively small place, much like a country estate, run by a well-organized, though not particularly intelligent, force of greater and lesser demons who require the Devil's help only when something out of the ordinary occurs. Babbitt's cover illustrations for both *The Devil's Storybook* and its sequel depict a neatly barbered Satan, dressed in what might be a comfortable, black polyester leisure suit, reading from a large book, which is recognizable as that which the reader holds in his or her hands. In both illustrations, the Devil appears quite content, in a good humor in fact. His legs are comfortably crossed, and his tail curves easily beneath a high-backed chair with flowered upholstery. In the cover illustration for *The Devil's Other Storybook,* a copy of the earlier volume lies at his feet. Although published some thirteen years apart, the books seem remarkably of a piece.

The Devil's Storybook

The first tale in *The Devil's Storybook,* the delightful "Wishes," is typical of a number of the pieces in the collection. "One day," it begins, "when things were dull in Hell,"[2] the Devil decides to go out and make mischief. The tone of this opening immediately tells us that Babbitt's Satan is a dilettante. Far from being the all-seeing tempter, forever watching each of us, he is, rather, the somewhat lackadaisical gentleman farmer of the Southey poem. The Devil's primary concern is for his own pleasure, and, like a gentleman farmer, he is interested in his "stock," humanity, only as the whim takes him.

In "Wishes" the Devil disguises himself as a fairy godmother and goes out into the world with no plan other than to make mischief by granting wishes, presumably wishes that will turn out badly for his victims. The magical wish that backfires is a motif that can be traced at least as far back as the Greek myth of Tithonus, whose lover, the goddess Eos, begged immortality for him from Zeus, but forgot to ask for eternal youth. (Tithonus thus lived on and on, getting older and more decrepit, until Eos changed him into a cricket.) In Babbitt's story, however, such wishes tend to cause problems not for the intended victims, but for the Devil himself. When he offers a wish to a grumpy farm wife, she responds, "Here's my wish. Since I don't believe in fairy godmothers, I wish you'd go back where you came from and leave me alone," which immediately sends him back to Hell where he "land[s] with a bump in his throne room" (*DS,* 4). Returning to the world, the Devil meets the pessimistic farm wife's virtual opposite, a happy old man who angers the Devil by refusing to make a wish because he is too contented with his life to want things to be different.

Only at the story's end does the Devil succeed in pulling off his practical joke and that success is trivial. He meets a vain young man who, upon hearing the presumed fairy godmother's offer, cannot decide what he wants and accidentally loses his chance by requesting that "she" tell him what to wish for. The Devil responds that the best possible choice would be "to wish that every wish [you] ever wish will always come true" (*DS,* 10), but then points out that by asking for help, the young man has used up the wish he had been promised. The Devil, his joke a success, returns to Hell, "well satisfied at last" (*DS,* 11), though the reader quickly realizes that the Devil's cleverness has actually caused him to lose by this exchange. If he had urged the vain young man to pick one of the earlier choices he had been mulling over—wealth, women, rulership of the world—the fellow would undoubtedly have put his soul in greater jeopardy than it now is.

In two other stories in the same vein, "The Power of Speech" and "Nuts," the Devil again acts from primarily selfish and petty motives. In the former story the Devil wants a goat named Walpurgis but is unable to steal him because his owner has hung a bell around the animal's neck. The Devil tries to tempt the woman, even offering to make her "Queen of the World," but she refuses because, as she says, "I've got my cottage, my goat and everything I need. . . . Why should I want to buy trouble? There's nothing you can do for me" (*DS,* 94). The Devil, however, knows that Walpurgis hates the bell around his neck and gives the animal the power of speech so that he can complain loudly and obscenely to his owner. The woman warns the goat that without the bell he will be stolen, but the goat, unable to think beyond the moment, insists on its removal. Needless to say, the Devil immediately takes the goat to Hell. As in "Wishes," however, Satan's triumph is only partial. Walpurgis continues to possess a vile temper and drives the Devil to a frenzy by making loud bell-ringing noises. In response, Satan transforms him into a stuffed goat and returns him to the old woman.

In "Nuts" we are told that the Devil loves walnuts, but hates to crack them, and hits upon the idea of tricking someone else to do it for him. Placing a pearl inside one walnut, he disguises himself as an old man and, meeting a farm wife, offers her the specially prepared nut. He assumes that, finding the pearl, she will then open all of the other nuts in the hope of finding another. When the farm wife merely eats her walnut and goes upon her way, however, the Devil is mystified. Assuming that he gave her the wrong nut by mistake, he cracks all of the others, looking for the pearl, but does not find it. Worse yet, having eaten all the meats, he ends up with a stomachache. The pearl, we learn, was in the first nut. The farm wife had realized what it was, saved it under her tongue, and left, uninterested in finding another. Later, Babbitt tells us, she "traded it for two turnips and a butter churn and went home again well pleased" (*DS,* 51). Shrewd enough to accept what she receives without comment and content, like the old man in "Wishes," with what she has, the farm wife is not moved by greed and is therefore proof against the Devil's lures. Her soul is in no jeopardy, and, even more upsetting to Babbitt's Devil, his practical joke turns against him.

Indeed, the ensnarement of souls seems to play little part in this Devil's agenda. In most cases, those whose souls belong to him simply appear at his gate without prodding and, seemingly little affected by their deaths, take up residence, much as if they were checking into a second-class resort hotel. Babbitt even implies that some of them—through their own actions rather than through predestination—have been more or less damned from a very early age; Basil and Jack of "The Harps of Heaven," for example, are "a pair of mean, low quarrelsome fellows who hated each other right from the start. . . . They had begun to fight when they were babies and fought all their lives" (*DS*, 21). Though the Devil does put temptation in the path of a living person in a number of Babbitt's stories, "Wishes" and "Nuts" for example, there is almost never anything systematic about his actions, and he rarely follows through on them. His primary interest lies in the pleasure of the temptation itself and in the practical joke that is often behind it. With very few exceptions, the long-range results of that temptation seem almost irrelevant to him. Nor are Satan's wiles particularly deep or seductive. Those who fall for his tricks invariably do so out of their own greed or vanity. Babbitt subtly emphasizes this fact in her illustrations. The Devil is a master of disguise, but whether he takes the shape of a fairy godmother in "Wishes," a peasant in "Nuts," or a mouse in "The Power of Speech," his tail is always visible, a dead giveaway to Babbitt's audience and, in some cases, to the characters being tempted that the situation is a setup.

When Babbitt portrays a character as damned and in Hell it is usually clear both that the damnation was deserved and that the punishment is suitable. Not only are her damned characters insufferable, but they are almost totally unaware of or at least unrepentant of their own faults. Oddly, their punishments, as often as not, are arrived at through what appears to be chance rather than through the Devil's conscious planning. A fitting punishment may or may not be assigned to a newly-arrived soul, apparently depending largely on whether or not the soul makes a nuisance of himself. Basil and Jack, in "The Harps of Heaven," a pair of professional thieves, enter Hell at just the moment when the Devil needs a bit of thievery done. A piano teacher, recently damned for nagging, has been complaining that there is no good music in Hell, which has upset the Devil, so he sends Basil and Jack to Heaven to steal a harp. They quickly discover that harps, like Grace, are free for the asking but, unable to control their predilection for fighting with each other, they end up damaging the instrument on their way home. The Devil sends them back twice more, always with the same result, a broken harp. Finally, Satan admits failure and, on the spur of the moment, comes up with an eminently suitable punishment. He makes Basil and Jack take piano lessons from the nagging piano teacher, "thereby punishing her as well, since the lessons went on for hundreds of years and the brothers never could learn anything but scales, no matter how much they practiced" (DS, 35).

Not only are the damned unaware of their faults, but some of them are so egocentric that they are unaware that they are even being punished. Typical of the stories in which we meet a damned soul is "Ashes," which concerns "a very bad man . . . a certain Mr. Bezzle, who made a great deal of money by cheating shamefully" (DS, 63). Upon his death Mr. Bezzle's body is cremated, but, by accident, his ashes are eventually mixed with those of a fireplace and a pork bone. The upshot is that in Hell Mr. Bezzle's spirit is followed everywhere by the spirit of a large and overaffectionate pig. Before the advent of the pig, Mr. Bezzle was thoroughly enjoying himself in Hell—"Everything's gone along well since I came down. Good company, plenty to eat and drink, a nice room all to myself" (DS, 66)—but the pig's attentions are making him miserable.

To be "stomach to stomach with a pig" (DS, 66) for eternity would seem a fitting end for Bezzle, but Babbitt makes it clear that the punishment is none of the Devil's doing. Indeed he needs to call in help to discover the cause of the animal's obsession. Nor does the Devil take exception to the preemptory way in which Bezzle insists that something be done. Rather, he immediately goes up to the World and returns with Bezzle's funeral urn. Although the dead man at first tries to separate his ashes from the pig's, by the story's end he has learned to "live" with the situation and has, in fact, made friends with the pig, whom he eventually teaches to cheat at cards.

Another reappearing plot device is the evil deed that accidentally causes good. In "The Very Pretty Lady," the first story Babbitt wrote for the book, and the one she likes the least,[3] a young woman remains unwed because she worries that her many suitors want her only for her beauty. Despite the wisdom this shows, the woman is also very proud of her good looks and spends considerable time in front of her mirror. Attracted by stories of her beauty, and deciding "that she was the very thing he needed to brighten up his days in Hell" (*DS*, 14), the Devil tries to tempt her into agreeing to return home with him, even though it is before her time. His lure is the promise that in Hell she can be eternally beautiful. The woman, however, has the wisdom to ask if there is love in Hell and, learning that there is not, rejects the Devil's offer. Angry because he cannot have her, Satan takes her beauty instead and "tack[s] it up in little fragments all over his throne room, where it sparkle[s] and twinkle[s] and brighten[s] up the place very nicely" (*DS*, 19–20). Years later, returning to check on the woman, he discovers her to be as ugly as he expected, but happily married to an equally ugly man who dotes on her. His trick has backfired.

Occasionally the Devil's tricks do work, however, and not only when played upon the damned. In "Perfection," a story widely praised by reviewers as "one of the more sophisticated tales" in *The Devil's Storybook*,[4] a little girl, appropriately named Angela, gains the Devil's ire by being too perfect and is therefore subjected by him to a series of Job-like torments: "He arranged for a cow to step on her favorite doll . . . [and] fixed it so that for weeks on end her cocoa was always too hot and her oatmeal too cold" (*DS*, 74). Nothing seems to faze the girl, who forgives the cow and, Babbitt tells us with a hint of irony, likes the torments because they "gave her a chance to show just how perfect she was" (*DS*, 74). Showing unusual staying power, the Devil continues to torment Angela without success for years. Eventually, however, he does succeed in cracking her veneer of perfection by arranging for her to get "a perfect husband and a perfect house and then [sending] her a fair-to-middling child" (*DS*, 77). In some ways the story reads like a variation on the parable of the pharisee and the tax collector, but a variation designed for those of us who, lacking Christ-like patience, would prefer to see a holier-than-thou type get hers on Earth rather than in Heaven. As Babbitt has written elsewhere, "It is often frustrating to follow the advice of Hamlet's father's ghost when he says of Queen Gertrude, 'Leave her to Heaven.' This is rather sophisticated advice, and not very satisfying" ("Moral Dilemmas," 6).

Although most of the tales in *The Devil's Storybook* conclude happily, at least for those who deserve happiness, several of the stories are somewhat ambiguous in their attitudes toward right and wrong, and these are worth examining separately. In "The Imp in the Basket," an oddly satisfying tale in which the Devil himself never appears, a clergyman discovers a baby in a basket on the steps of his church and decides to raise it as his own. In many folktales involving foster children, it later becomes apparent that the baby is a changeling rather than human, but in Babbitt's version, the clergyman realizes that the child is an imp, a devil's baby, from the first. Despite second thoughts and the condemnation of his parishioners, he nonetheless decides to raise the child because, he reasons, "A baby is a baby—helpless and in need of protection . . . perhaps the imp can be raised in the ways of goodness" (*DS*, 38–44). The villagers take exception to this attitude, however, and, deciding that the clergyman himself is damned, set fire to his cottage, intending to burn both minister and imp. The fire, of course, pleases the imp who immediately disappears, leaving the clergyman miraculously unburned in the ashes of the cottage. He returns to his old life, but is never sure whether he has been saved from death by God, by the imp, or by the Devil himself. A smudge of soot is found on the church steps where the imp's basket had rested and proves impossible to wash away. Ironically, a pot of sickly ivy placed to hide the smudge immediately begins to flourish. Babbitt leaves both the clergyman and her readers up in the air as to whether the miracles involved in the story are God's work or the Devil's.

Similarly ambiguous, but less satisfying, is "A Palindrome," in which a warm, kindhearted artist gains fame for painting hideously ugly pictures of people doing awful things to each other. The Devil, envying those pictures, steals them one night, hoping that the loss of his work will so embitter the artist that he will turn to evil and thus become a candidate for Hell. It should be noted, however, that the Devil's primary purpose here is not to gain a damned soul but to gain a court painter. Unable to afford art supplies, the painter turns to digging ditches for a living and becomes embittered. Eventually, he does return to art, this time as a sculptor. Unlike his paintings, his statues are all works of beauty—mothers with children, religious icons—but this appears to have no effect on his steadily worsening temperament. Babbitt tells us that "it seemed as if all the good in the artist came out in his work and left behind nothing but evil in the man himself" (*DS*, 60). The Devil is pleased by the degeneration of the artist's personality but upset by his choice of uplifting subject matter. Evidently unconcerned about the possibility of gaining the man's soul, the Devil loses interest in him when his art ceases to please. In the end we never learn what happened to the man himself. "His paintings are admired in Hell . . . his statues are admired in Heaven, but the man himself seems to have been lost somewhere in between" (*DS*, 61).

Perhaps because the tales in *The Devil's Storybook* are short and almost invariably humorous, one is tempted to see the book as minor, as a resting place between the author's major literary efforts. The work falls chronologically between Babbitt's longest children's novel, *Goody Hall*, and her acknowledged masterpiece, *Tuck Everlasting. The Devil's Storybook,* however, has sold well and has been widely praised by reviewers. Joyce Alpern Young, in *Kirkus Reviews,* writes of the book in glowing terms, saying "Natalie Babbitt's traditional themes abound in elegant twists, and she polishes even the straightest to a pleasing, most un-Angelic perfection."[5] The *Bulletin of the Center for Children's Books* sees "some variation in the solidity of the plots," but states that "the quiet humor and vitality of the writing style are ubiquitous."[6] *The Devil's Storybook* was a finalist for the National

Book Award in 1975, was named an American Library Association Notable Book, and won the Lewis Carroll Shelf Award.

Furthermore, the collection is thematically consistent with Babbitt's major novels. Like them, it establishes a middle ground between the sugary-sweet optimism so common in earlier children's literature and the almost neurotic blackness of the supposedly realistic children's fiction of recent decades. *The Devil's Storybook* also attempts to avoid the oversimplified, virtually absolute black and white of much children's literature on the subject of evil. Babbitt's Devil is clearly a bad person, but he is hardly the monster of fundamentalist Christianity. If his badness seems somewhat watered down from that portrayed in other books that attempt to demonstrate to children the existence of evil in the world, and if his actions often bring ambiguous and somewhat ironic results, this is to Babbitt's credit. Few children, after all, have any very great interest in or understanding of the adult versions of the seven deadly sins that are often pressed upon them, but they can understand a nagging piano teacher, a petty devil, or the almost overwhelming compulsion to fight with brothers and sisters.

It can thus be argued that the very pettiness of the evil portrayed in *The Devil's Storybook* brings the concept of right and wrong close to the book's intended readers and strips that evil of any glamour they might otherwise find in it. Children know themselves to be capable of evil and, furthermore, occasionally find themselves in situations where it is hard for them to believe that their supposedly evil impulses are entirely bad. Many of us, as children, knew a little girl like Angela and hated her for her perfection. We may even have felt the urge to do something— pick a fight, say something nasty, break a beloved toy—simply to mar that perfection. That the Devil's motives are not always clear even to himself, that he is often moved by the need to satisfy his own selfish urges rather than by any real desire to perpetrate major badness, and that his actions often leave him looking ridiculous accurately reflect the nature of evil as every child knows it to exist in our everyday world.

Equally important, however, is the positive note struck in so many of the stories. Since the Devil simply does not work very hard at tempting people, those who are punished in *The Devil's Storybook* can invariably be seen as deserving it; they are never portrayed as essentially good people who have been tricked into sin. Ironically, this allows the reader to see the Devil in many of the stories as a positive, or at least useful, character, handing out poetic justice. In *The Devil's Storybook* evil exists and punishment is a real possibility, but sensible people can avoid both. The old man in "Wishes," because he is satisfied with his life, is beyond the Devil's reach. Despite a tendency toward vanity, the protagonist of "The Very Pretty Lady" is able to resist temptation, as are a number of other characters in the stories. Even for those sentenced permanently to Hell a certain amount of happiness is possible. Basil and Jack could have had a heavenly harp—the joy of it was theirs for the asking—but they chose to act in a manner that led to its destruction. In "Ashes" Bezzle and his pig actually become friends. Even the title character of "The Rose and the Minor Demon"—who by his very nature is presumably more thoroughly damned than are former human beings like Basil, Jack, and Bezzle—can achieve a compromise and find happiness in Hell. This demon, who Babbitt tells us is "a wistful, sentimental creature who really didn't belong in Hell at all" (*DS*, 79), discovers in the Devil's treasure room a porcelain vase painted with roses and, moved by the beauty of it, asks permission to plant a rose garden in Hell. The Devil, scandalized, refuses, but does agree to let the demon plant more appropriate things like henbane and hemlock. Disobeying the Devil, the demon plants a rosebush as well. Satan soon discovers it and orders both the rosebush destroyed and the vase painted black. Later, however, when the vase is broken, the black paint chips off, and the demon is able to hide a fragment of it under his pillow; "knowing it was there . . . made the minor demon happy in a small and secret way that no one ever knew about but him" (*DS*, 89).

In *The Devil's Storybook* Satan and evil are real, but the Devil is a petty, somewhat ridiculous fellow, and his power is far from absolute. Babbitt shows us this in a manner likely to be both clear and entertaining to adults as well as children. In the final analysis, it is only by refusing to be aware of our own behavior and by refusing to take responsibility for our actions that we give the Devil any control over us. Resolute human beings of any age can resist or outwit Satan or, more important, the evil within themselves. Even Satan's own minions have some control over their fate, and beauty can continue to exist, unbeknownst to the Devil, in the depths of Hell itself.

The Devil's Other Storybook

Like Natalie Babbitt's earlier collection, *The Devil's Other Story-book* (1987) is a delightful but relatively minor work, especially considered in the light of the masterful adult novel *Herbert Rowbarge,* which preceded it. The book opens with a repetition of the lines from Southey's "The Devil's Walk," which began Babbitt's previous collection, but then adds the second stanza from the same poem:

> Over the hill and over the dale,
>   And he went over the plain;
> And backward and forward he swished his tail,
>   As a gentleman swishes a cane.

The emphasis, once again, is on the Devil as country squire and dilettante, officially overseeing his estate, but primarily on a pleasure jaunt.

Babbitt's new collection is similar to *The Devil's Storybook* in form, though somewhat less lighthearted. The wonderful first tale in the volume, "The Fortunes of Madame Organza," is, in a sense, a variation on the opening story of the earlier book. In "Wishes" the Devil intended to grant people their hearts' desires, doing so in such a way as to make them suffer. In "The Fortunes of Madame Organza" he sets about to make the predictions of a second-rate fortune-teller come true. The woman, however, is not very original and tends to predict over and over that people will find a pot of gold, take a long journey, or meet the proverbial tall, dark stranger. As Babbitt describes it, "during the days that followed, thanks to the Devil's interference, the village changed completely. Twenty-two people found pots of gold and went to live in the city, which they soon found dismal to the utmost but were too proud to say so. Another thirty-seven went off on long journeys, ending up in such spots as Borneo and Peru with no way at all to get back, and so they were forced, for a living, to chop bamboo or to keep herds of llamas in the Andes."[7] Everyone else meets tall, dark strangers "who hung about, getting in the way, and looking altogether so alarming in their black hats and cloaks and their long black beards that the villagers remaining were afraid to stay and hurried to move in with relatives in other villages, which caused no end of bad feelings" (*DOS*, 8–9).

Madame Organza eventually runs out of business since none of the strangers want their fortunes told (they are too busy taking care of abandoned farm animals). Switching professions, she does their laundry, all of which, Babbitt tells us, is black. Although the moral of "The Fortunes of Madame Organza" is an old and obvious one—be careful about what you wish for because you might get it—it needs restating periodically, especially so in this age of instant-winner state lotteries and come-in-the-mail, million-dollar sweepstakes.

Several of the tales in *The Devil's Other Storybook* are reminiscent of "Ashes" and "The Harps of Heaven" from the earlier volume, demonstrating the ways in which the damned find their own punishments in Hell. In "Boating," a group of newly arrived old ladies refuses to leave the boat they have taken over the river Styx because "we can't imagine what we're doing here with all these common types" (*DOS*, 27). The Devil, who is helping Charon out because ferry traffic is backed up, is annoyed by their belief in their own superiority and decides to leave them in the boat, floating on the river Styx forever. In "Simple Sentences" a thief who speaks in slang and a snob who speaks in pompous euphemisms enter Hell together, both having died in the scuffle that resulted when the former attempted to rob the latter. The two will

Illustration from *The Devil's Storybook* by Natalie Babbitt. © 1974. *Reprinted by permission of Farrar, Straus & Giroux.*

not stop quarreling, however, so the Devil, his patience tried by their abuse of the language, sentences them to be put together in a room designed for one "til it all freezes over down here" (*DOS*, 71). In yet another story, "Justice," a big-game hunter, appropriately named Bangs, is sentenced to spend eternity hunting and being hunted by a rhinoceros. As in "Boating," "The Harps of Heaven," and the other stories of this type, it is clear that the Devil comes up with this punishment spontaneously. Nothing is planned. It just happens that a rhinoceros is terrorizing certain parts of Hell when Bangs turns up, so the Devil puts the two of them together on the spur of the moment.

On the other hand, in "The Sign Post," as in "The Very Pretty Lady," the Devil accidentally does good while attempting evil. In this story two romantically inclined, but ill-suited young lovers quarrel almost continually and decide to separate. The young man, Gil, tells his girlfriend, Flora, where he will be for the next week and suggests that "if you can promise you'll never argue again, send me a message and I'll come back and marry you" (*DOS*, 41). Flora does send the message a few days later, but the Devil, acting out of pure maliciousness and not even knowing about Gil and Flora, has changed the signposts on the road, causing Flora's messenger to go astray. Meanwhile, Gil too has had a change of heart and now wants Flora back. Since neither lover gets a response to his or her message, however, each assumes that the other is no longer interested. This destroys a relationship that probably would not have worked out in any case and leaves them free to find other, more suitable mates and live happily ever after.

In "The Soldier," "Lessons," and "How Akbar Went to Bethlehem," the Devil puts on a disguise, as he did in "Wishes" and "Nuts" in *The Devil's Storybook*. In the first of these stories he appears as an old man with a crutch and confronts a soldier who, because no war is going on, is busy keeping up his spirits by practicing his marching. The story differs from those in *The Devil's Storybook*, however, in that the Devil neither plays a practical joke upon the soldier not tries seriously to tempt him, although he does work on the man's ego a bit, complimenting him on "what an elegant picture you make" (*DOS*, 19). For the most part he is content to listen as the soldier names the famous battles he has been in, the Devil's only response throughout this listing being an antiphonal "I was there." It is clear that there is no need for the Devil to tempt the fellow. The soldier assumes that the old man who claims to have been at all the world's great battles is merely senile, but the reader realizes the truth of the matter. Surely, any time men kill their fellows in great numbers Satan must be involved in it. The soldier, who kills professionally and loves his work, is already damned. The Devil does not have to tempt him. All he need do is wait.

In both "Lessons" and "How Akbar Went to Bethlehem," however, the Devil suffers frustration. In the former story, when he appears at an old woman's gate disguised as a strolling musician, he encounters the woman's parrot, Columbine, who, unfortunately for Satan, had previously lived with a clergyman. The parrot, who we are told "liked things on the up-and-up" (*DOS,* 47), sees through the disguise and raises such a racket that everyone hides or runs away, thus spoiling the Devil's plans. Indeed, despite his success with the rhinoceros in "Justice," the Devil's record in his encounters with animals is not a good one. In his attempt to steal Walpurgis the goat he achieves at best a draw. Columbine the parrot absolutely routs him. Equally unsuccessful is his confrontation with Akbar the camel.

At the beginning of "Akbar," Babbitt notes that "there are no camels in Hell. [Though] you might suppose there would be, for camels have shocking bad tempers" (*DOS,* 33). Once long ago, however, there was a camel in Hell named Akbar who was the Devil's special pet. Then one night the Devil saw a strange light in the sky and, disguising himself as an Arab, went to investigate it. The light, of course, was the Star of Bethlehem. Akbar engaged the Devil's everlasting hatred by first bowing to the Magi as they passed on their own camels—incidentally pitching the Devil off his back—and then following them to get a look at the Christ child, something the Devil feared to do. Although the rhinoceros in "Justice" seems to be little more than a force of nature, the other animals that appear in Babbitt's stories are very human and, like humans, must stand or fall on the basis of their innate

Illustration from *The Devil's Other Storybook* by Natalie Babbitt. © 1987.
Reprinted by permission of Farrar, Straus & Giroux.

ability to make moral choices. The goat Walpurgis in "The Power of Speech," because he is primarily concerned with his own immediate comfort, ends up first in Hell and then stuffed on his owner's front lawn. Both Akbar the camel and Columbine the parrot prove themselves capable of choosing more wisely.

The two remaining tales in *The Devil's Other Storybook* both seem to show the Devil in a positive light. "The Fall and Rise of Bathbone" concerns a "little, sweet no one of a man" (*DOS*, 53), Bathbone, who suffers from the delusion that he is an opera singer named Doremi Faso. When the real Faso dies he immediately goes to Hell for a number of good reasons. Bathbone, however, upon learning of Faso's death in the newspaper, is so surprised that he accidentally falls off a bridge. He too ends up in Hell, not because he deserves to be there, but because Heaven decides that he "had better go to Hell and get himself straight as to who he really was. For in Heaven they like you to know that kind of thing and be content with it" (*DOS*, 55). It would seem logical for the Devil to be glad of any soul that comes his way, but this is not the case. Rather, he decides to convince Bathbone that he does not belong in Hell by setting up a concert for him, complete with orchestra and audience. Hearing his own voice, realizing that he is a tenor and not a bass like Faso, Bathbone recovers his identity, regains his sense of self-worth, and is immediately taken up to Heaven where he happily enrolls in a glee club.

In "The Ear," the most complex piece in *The Devil's Other Storybook*, the Devil does not appear directly, as he doesn't in "The Imp in the Basket" from *The Devil's Storybook*. In the earlier piece, the entire story is highly ambiguous, and we are never really sure whether God or Satan is responsible for the miracles. Something similar occurs in "The Ear."

The story concerns a rather slow and immature young man named Beevis, whose parents have no respect for him. One day, while digging a well, Beevis discovers the buried head of a gigantic idol, a rather funny-looking and useless idol, Babbitt tells us, left over from long ago, which had been built and rather unsuccessfully worshipped by "a clan of very silly people called the Pishpash" (*DOS*, 73). Since he never finishes digging it up, it would be more accurate, perhaps, to say that Beevis discovers the idol's ear, "big as a washtub" (*DOS*, 76) at the bottom of his hole. A minor earthquake occurs as he and his parents stand looking down at the ear, and they, taking this for an omen, tell him to cover it back up. Beevis pretends to do so, but merely hides the hole and secretly begins to visit it late each night to tell it his troubles. This gives him increased confidence and improved posture, and it makes him seem an altogether more intelligent person. Eventually just as his parents are about to discover that Beevis is talking to the ear, another earthquake occurs, causing them to move elsewhere. Beevis, however, decides to stay by his ear, becomes a successful farmer, and lives happily ever after. Each night he continues to talk to the ear, telling it "his hopes and joys," and, Babbitt tells us, "every night the ear heard every word" (*DOS*, 82).

The Devil is mentioned only once in "The Ear," in connection with the Pishpash whose silliness, we are told, he found entertaining. The story, therefore, could easily be interpreted as a more or less realistic piece of fiction. Beevis thinks that the ear is listening to him and, because he has "someone" to talk to, he begins to formulate ideas more intelligently, gain self-respect, and mature. Within the context of *The Devil's Other Storybook,* however, it is hard to believe that the ear, conveying Beevis's words below as it does, is not in some sense the Devil's own ear. Although Beevis never receives an explicit answer to anything he says, the earthquakes seem to come at singularly appropriate moments. An earlier quake tumbled the idol and sent the Pishpash packing. Other quakes buried the idol. Two final quakes saw to it that Beevis's parents stayed away from the ear and that they eventually left him alone with it. But, in spite of the implicit connection between the Ear and the underworld, there is no indication of anything negative in the story. Indeed, at the tale's end, Beevis is a much better person in every way. If he does in fact have the Devil's ear, it has done him only good. Although many of the tales in *The Devil's Storybook* and its sequel seem decidedly Christian in their morality, "The Ear" is certainly not one of them. It is an ambiguous puzzler, a story to be returned to and thought about.

As stated earlier, Babbitt's two collections, though separated by thirteen years, really are of a piece and much of what was said about *The Devil's Storybook* therefore applies equally to *The Devil's Other Storybook*. When asked if her outlook on life has changed over the years, Babbitt has stated that "my 'world view' has not so much changed as solidified, as a direct result of aging and experience,"[8] and the strong thematic ties between these two collections seem to bear out this statement. It can be argued that *The Devil's Other Storybook* is somewhat better written than the earlier work—Babbitt's style is fractionally tighter, her humor a bit more pointed, her plots a trifle more sophisticated—but her purpose is the same. Both books use humor and irony to portray a Devil who is at once worth worrying about and a bit ridiculous. Both books tell us that evil does exist, but reassure us that we are in control.

6

To Live Forever
Tuck Everlasting

Far and away Babbitt's most popular novel, and in the opinion of her critics her best, *Tuck Everlasting* (1975) has received numerous honors, most importantly the Christopher Award in 1976.[1] It has also appeared on any number of recommended lists, including those of the International Board on Books for Young People, the American Library Association, and the *School Library Journal*. Furthermore, *Tuck Everlasting* was probably the single most important factor in Babbitt's receiving the George G. Stone Award for her life's work in children's literature in 1979. The book thus qualifies as one of a small number of acknowledged classics in the field. Set as it is in an almost timeless, premodern America, free as it is from the trendy hyperrealism that was just beginning to dominate the field of children's literature in the mid-seventies, *Tuck Everlasting* should be able to hold its position as a classic indefinitely.

Tuck Everlasting is set in the summer of 1881. Babbitt never mentions a location in the novel, but had in mind a cross between the heavily forested frontier of Conrad Richter's Ohio pioneer trilogy *The Awakening Land,* a region her own ancestors had been instrumental in settling, and the Adirondack foothills of upstate New York where she lived while her husband was serving as president of Kirkland College.[2] Winnie Foster, the novel's eleven-year-old protagonist, lives in a prim and proper cottage with a fenced-in yard on the edge of the town of Treegap. Her family, among the region's earliest settlers, is very clearly gentry, and Winnie, like Willet in *Goody Hall,* is most definitely not encouraged to play with the other, less affluent children of the town. Just beyond the iron fence that circles Winnie's "touch-me-not" cottage,[3] rises the mysterious Treegap wood. It is not very large, and the Fosters are under the impression that they own it. Like the woldweller's forest in *The Search for Delicious,* however, the wood is magic and beyond the ownership of anyone. Like the Old Forest in Tolkien's *The Lord of the Rings,* it is a fragment of something very ancient, something left over, perhaps, from an earlier creation.

In *The Search for Delicious,* the woldweller, protector of the forest lives in a tree at the exact center of that forest, a particularly magical place. At the exact center of the Treegap wood is an ancient and gigantic ash tree. In 1794, Angus and Mae Tuck, with their two sons, pioneers traveling westward, camped by the ash tree in the heart of what was then a continent-spanning forest. They and their horse drank from the spring and moved on, unaware that their lives had been changed forever. Years later, however, it became apparent that none of them had aged since that day. The Tucks were humble folk, and immortality at first had a rather minimal effect on their day-to-day life-style. Most drastically affected was the elder of the Tuck children, Miles. After several decades, his mortal wife, realizing that he had not aged, decided that he had made a deal with the devil and left him. He seems the most bitter of the Tucks. His parents, on the other hand, seem mostly just tired and a bit depressed, unable to come to terms with what has happened to them, unable to find any way to profit from it, but certain that it must be kept a secret. In contrast, their younger son, Jesse, although a 104-year-old as the book opens, maintains the open-minded enthusiasm of the seventeen-year-old boy he was when he drank the water of immortality.

Although Babbitt does not use the name, she clearly implies a connection between the Tuck's ash tree and Yggdrasil, the wondrous ash tree of Norse mythology, which, according to tradition, supported the entire universe. At the base of one root of Yggdrasil lay Urda's Well, protected by the Norns, its water "so holy that none might drink of it."[4] The primary duty of the Norns was to determine men and women's fates, and thus the length of their lives. At the base of another root lay the Well of Knowledge, protected by Mimir, God of Wisdom. The parallel with the trees in the Garden of Eden seems obvious. Central to the myth of Yggdrasil, however, and to the entire, doom-laden Norse mythology, was the paradoxical idea of limited immortality. The tree, like the Norse gods, was immortal and yet, like them, could die. Gnawing at its roots were serpents that would someday bring it crashing down and end the world.[5]

Like Yggdrasil, the ash tree in the Treegap woods has water at its base, in this case a small spring, and, like Urda's Well, the Treegap spring confers eternal life. It should be noted, however, that there is nothing at the base of the tree comparable to Mimir's Well; the spring bestows the immortality of the gods, but not their wisdom. In Norse myth, unending life, the prerogative of the gods, is seen as inherently good, and the eventual death of the Norse gods is a great tragedy. In Greek myth, immortality is seen in a similar positive light; unending life is, in most cases, the greatest boon the gods can give a mortal.[6] Christianity's emphasis on life after death expresses, perhaps, a similar belief that the winning of eternity is a great prize. Natalie Babbitt, however, is not sure that this is true. To an extent, *Tuck Everlasting* can be seen as her attempt to examine both sides of what is for her a very complex question, with the Tuck family and Winnie Foster as her primary tools.

When Winnie Foster discovers Jesse at the spring and attempts to drink from it herself, he panics. Although the Tucks have known that some day they would be faced with a situation much like this, they have never developed a plan for dealing with it. On the spur of the moment, Jesse and his mother kidnap Winnie and take her cross-country to the rundown old shack where Angus and Mae have been living for the last twenty years. By coincidence, however, they are seen by a stranger to Treegap whom

Babbitt calls "the man in the yellow suit." He, we discover, has been searching for the Tucks for many years, ever since as a child his grandmother told him stories she had heard from Miles's wife, stories about "people who never grew older" (*TE*, 95).

These events set up the central conflict of *Tuck Everlasting*. There is a spring in the woods whose water confers immortality on anyone who drinks from it. Should this be made public knowledge? Angus, Mae, and Miles want to keep it a secret, not out of greed, but because they consider their immortality a curse. Angus Tuck argues that life is like a great turning wheel: "Everything's a wheel, turning and turning, never stopping. The frogs is part of it, and the bugs, and the fish. . . . And people. But never the same ones. Always coming in new, always growing and changing, and always moving on. That's the way it's supposed to be. That's the way it *is*" (*TE*, 62). They, however, have fallen off the wheel and, to their eternal sorrow, have been left behind. Jesse Tuck, on the other hand, is more optimistic about the experience and, sounding almost like Peter Pan,[7] asks Winnie to join him when she grows up. "We could get married. . . . We could have a grand old time, go all around the world, see everything. Listen, Ma and Pa and Miles, they don't know how to enjoy it, what we got. . . . you and me, we could have a good time that never, never stopped." (*TE*, 72).

For the man in the yellow suit the spring is clearly an overwhelming temptation to do evil. Having blackmailed the Foster family into giving him the deed to the Treegap wood in exchange for his promise that he will rescue Winnie, he goes to retrieve her from the Tucks. He has, however, no intention of returning the girl to her family. Not only does he want to drink from the spring himself, but he also plans to force Winnie to do so, without first giving her a chance to grow up. Trapped in an eternal childhood, she would become little more than a sideshow freak, a moneymaking advertisement of the water's power. Equally wicked, the stranger plans to sell the water only to the rich and powerful.

What would it be like to live forever? Immortality is one of the standard wish-fulfillment fantasies, and the more simplistic visions of it that can be culled from myth and literature generally include either the assumption of a transcendent wisdom that will eliminate all the problems of our current lives or a sort of never-ending summer vacation, an Elysium of fun and games. But what if immortality simply froze people at the age they were when they drank from the fountain, neither renewing their youth nor improving their defects? What would it be like to live forever as a poorly educated, rather limited and exceedingly tired middle-aged man; as a frustrated husband, forever separated from his family; as a naive and energetic adolescent, poised on the doorstep to adulthood, but never able to cross the threshold?

Angus Tuck is certain that immortality is a bad thing. His life since he realized that he would never age has consisted of little beyond drudgery and boredom. He and Mae spend some of their time—how much is unclear—making quilts, rugs, bowls, primitive toys, and other handicrafts, which they sell in various towns about the region to earn enough money to live on. The informal, catch-as-catch-can nature of their house, with its silver cobwebs and a mouse living in a drawer, has some charms for Winnie, who has spent all her life in a cottage where nothing is ever out of place, but she soon realizes that the house is actually a slovenly, decaying mess. From this, one gets the clear impression that the Tucks don't really work very hard. Depression governs their lives. Angus, we are told, "almost never smiled except in sleep" (*TE*, 9). Even then, his smiles are the result of a recurring dream of death, in which "we're all in heaven and never heard of Treegap" (*TE*, 10). On a daily basis, sleep seems to be virtually the only thing he has to look forward to with pleasure. For this reason, Winnie's appearance, even though it may spell disaster for his family, strikes him as "the finest thing that's happened in—oh—at least eighty years" (*TE*, 49). The Tucks live from day to day, lacking any real sense of purpose, and they have no expectations for the future. As Mae Tuck says to her husband, "It's no use having that dream. . . . Nothing's going to change" (*TE*, 10).

To the extent that the Tucks have a plan for dealing with Winnie after they kidnap her, it seems to consist of very little more than Angus's attempt to convince the girl that immortality is not a good thing and that it is necessary to keep the spring a secret.

Winnie, however, is at that watershed age when she is just beginning to see death as a real possibility, and she is adamant that
she does not want to die: "All at once her mind was drowned with
understanding of what he was saying. For she—yes, even she—
would go out of the world willy-nilly someday. Just go out, like
the flame of a candle, and no use protesting. It was a certainty.
She would try very hard not to think of it, but sometimes, as now,
it would be forced upon her. She raged against it, helpless and
insulted, and blurted at last, 'I don't want to die' " (*TE,* 63).

Angus, on the other hand, has no doubt that death serves a
useful purpose and, as his dream indicates, he would accept it
gladly:

> Dying's part of the wheel, right there next to being born.
> You can't pick out the pieces you like and leave the rest.
> Being part of the whole thing, that's the blessing. But it's
> passing us by, us Tucks. Living's heavy work, but off to
> one side the way *we* are, it's useless too. It don't make
> sense. If I knowed how to climb back on the wheel, I'd do
> it in a minute. You can't have living without dying. So
> you can't call it living, what we got. We just *are,* we just
> *be,* like rocks beside the road. (*TE,* 63–64).

Is Angus Tuck right? His arguments seem persuasive, and yet
his son Jesse clearly disagrees. Winnie finds Jesse enormously
attractive from the very beginning. She is just at the age where
she is beginning to find boys interesting, and Jesse, with his good
looks and outgoing personality, definitely tempts her to consider
sharing immortality with him. Fed up with the restrictions placed
upon her by her family, as symbolized by her grandmother's
nearly continuous fault finding and, especially, by the iron fence
that surrounds her cottage, the girl sees Jesse Tuck as enormously free, as able to do all the things she wishes she could do.
Natalie Babbitt, however, is on the side of Angus Tuck, and he
clearly functions as her voice in the novel.[8] Although she never,
within the book, explicitly contradicts Jesse's assertion that he
and Winnie could be happy as immortals, Babbitt has stated elsewhere that when she started writing *Tuck* she "felt that it would

be a bad thing to live forever. By the time I was finished with it, I thought it would be absolutely terrible. The boredom! One of the things which gives life its zest is that you know that it's not going to last."[9]

It also seems clear that, even if it could be shown that immortality would be a blessing for people with more intellectual flexibility than the Tucks, it would still pose an enormous threat to society.[10] The man in the yellow suit tells the Tucks that "ignorant people like you should never have the opportunity [to live forever]. It should be kept for . . . certain others. And for me" (*TE*, 98). The stranger plans to sell the water "only to certain people, people who deserve it. And it will be very, very expensive. But who wouldn't give a fortune to live forever?" (*TE*, 97–98). Possibly those who deserve it in his eyes will be, essentially, anyone who can afford to meet his price. Possibly he has another agenda. We know nothing of the stranger's politics or religion, but he is clearly a fanatic. Who but a fanatic, after all, could devote his entire life to a search for the Tucks based only on the stories of his grandmother, stories that he admits "took possession" (*TE*, 95) of him?

In response to the man in the yellow suit's threats, Mae Tuck kills him, smashing in his skull with the stock of a shotgun. Her act is unpremeditated. She does it to protect Winnie. When Mae picks up the gun, we are told that "her strong arms swung the shotgun round her head, like a wheel" (*TE*, 100).Throughout *Tuck Everlasting* the wheel has served as a symbol for the workings of nature, whether it be the turning of the seasons, or the necessary cycle of birth and death. Babbitt's choice of metaphor here implies that the death of the stranger is necessary. Though she may no longer be part of it, Mae Tuck acts as a representative of the natural order, which the stranger would have disrupted. From a legal point of view she has, perhaps, committed murder, but morally she is innocent of wrongdoing. Unfortunately for her, she kills the stranger just as the Treegap constable arrives on the scene. He cannot arrest the Tucks for kidnapping because Winnie insists that she went with them of her own free will, but he can and does arrest Mae.

Although there is some talk of hanging Mae Tuck for the crime of murder, it is important to realize that she personally is never

Cover illustration from *Tuck Everlasting* by Natalie Babbitt. © 1975. *Reprinted by permission of Farrar, Straus & Giroux.*

in any danger. The Tucks, after all, cannot be killed, as they know from past experience, having survived falls, snake bites, and point-blank shotgun blasts without a scratch. An attempted hanging, however, would expose their secret almost as completely as the man in the yellow suit would have. This places Winnie Foster in an unusual situation. Throughout her entire life she has been essentially a passive being, wanting to break away from her restrictive family, but unable to do so in any effective way. Natalie Babbitt sees this as a typical situation for children and has argued that, for the most part, "child heroes, like their flesh-and-blood counterparts, being powerless, innocent, and mainly unformed, are acted upon rather than acting."[11] Now, however, Winnie can act. When the Tucks break Mae out of jail, she volunteers to spend the night in the jail cell, wrapped in blankets, so that the constable will not realize his prisoner is gone until it is too late for pursuit. Her action is effective, the Tucks escape, and Winnie never sees them again.

While helping Mae Tuck escape, Winnie remembers two lines of poetry, "Stone walls do not a prison make, / Nor iron bars a cage," which "over and over . . . repeated themselves in her head till they were altogether meaningless" (*TE*, 123). Although Babbitt does not identify the poem, these are the first lines from the last stanza of Richard Lovelace's "To Althea, from Prison," written circa 1648. The entire stanza runs as follows:

> Stone walls do not a prison make,
>   Nor iron bars a cage;
> Minds innocent and quiet take
>   That for an hermitage;
> If I have freedom in my love,
>   And in my soul am free,
> Angels alone that soar above
>   Enjoy such liberty,[12]

Lovelace, a supporter of the defeated King Charles, a man used to thinking of himself as a privileged member of the upper class, has seen his entire world swept away by the English Civil War.

On the literal level he finds himself helpless, without power, imprisoned, and yet he insists that his mind and soul remain free because he retains the freedom to love.

Winnie, as a child, has also seen herself as powerless, and this has always bothered her. After her adventure with the Tucks, however, she no longer suffers from her previous frustration. Even though her family has been humiliated, even though her parents have tightened the restrictions upon her and have grounded her indefinitely, she actually looks forward to the near future: "School would open soon. It wouldn't be so bad. In fact, she thought as her spirits lifted, this year it might be rather nice" (*TE,* 130). Her love for the Tucks has made it possible for her to act in a meaningful fashion, and, because of this, her world has changed forever. Her mother and father can lay down as many rules and restrictions as they want, but Winnie now knows that she has choices and can make decisions on her own. When Winnie is the only one who can speak with straightforward honesty about the stranger's death and its effect on the Fosters' ownership of the Treegap wood, her parents dimly realize that their daughter has somehow gained a new maturity, that "she is different now from what she had been before" (*TE,* 107).

Winnie, however, has no real desire to isolate herself, as the Tucks have been isolated, from the rest of society, so she will, for the most part, follow her parents' and society's rules. But she will do so because she wants to, because she chooses to. The Tucks have unintentionally placed Winnie in a position where several times she has had to act contrary to the world's simplistic concept of right and wrong. She has had to lie, she has had to condone a murder, she has had to help a woman escape from jail, all actions that she is convinced are morally correct. Having done such things, Winnie is aware that she is capable of doing them again, if her conscience tells her that it is necessary. In short, she has reached what Lawrence Kohlberg, building on the work of Piaget, calls the "postconventional level" of moral development, that highest level of morality where "if a choice must be made between following an administrative order and keeping another human from inappropriate and unjust actions, the higher principles of justice and human rights take precedence over the rule."[13]

Ultimately, the most extreme manner in which Winnie could step outside of conventional boundries is for her to choose immortality, and she does consider doing so. Jesse has given her a small bottle of spring water, which he asks her to drink when she is seventeen. Instead, making her own choice, she pours it on a toad that she has been playing with in her yard, granting that humble creature life everlasting. This is not a simple rejection of immortality for, as she knows, "there was more water in the wood. . . . Just in case. When she was seventeen. If she should decide, there was more water in the wood. Winnie smiled" (*TE*, 132–33). At the age of eleven she knows that she is not yet ready to make such an important decision. In the epilogue, which takes place some seventy years later, we learn from her tombstone that Winnie Foster eventually decided to forgo immortality with Jesse Tuck, preferring to live a more normal life as wife and mother, dying at the age of seventy-eight. Angus Tuck, although saddened both by her death and by the pain her decision has caused his son Jesse, realizes that Winnie made the right choice: "Tuck wiped his eyes hastily. Then he straightened his jacket again and drew up his hand in a brief salute. 'Good girl,' he said aloud. And then he turned and left the cemetery" (*TE*, 138).

The Angus Tuck who visits Winnie's grave in the year 1950 seems entirely unchanged from his earlier self, though almost everything has changed around him. He drives the same, or a similar wooden wagon, pulled by the same tired old horse. He and his wife still travel the roads without real purpose, living nowhere for any great length of time. The town of Treegap, on the other hand, now boasts a gas station, a diner, and a hotel. The site of the Treegap wood is covered with houses. Three years earlier, Angus discovers, the big ash tree in the center of the woods "got hit by lightning, split right down the middle. Caught fire and everything. Tore up the ground, too. Had to bulldoze her out" (*TE*, 136). The spring of immortality is gone, destroyed, perhaps, by divine fire, and the danger that others will discover eternal life is presumably gone with it. The Tucks, their horse, and Winnie Foster's toad, still sitting by the road in 1950, are presumably the only beneficiaries of the water.

Earlier in her career Natalie Babbitt had argued that happy endings are a necessity in children's literature. For children, she suggested, "no matter how unpromising their circumstances, it is not too late" (Babbitt, "Happy Endings?" 158). Dick Foote, Phoebe, Gaylen, Egan, Willet, and Mylo all, so far as we know, live happily ever after. Even the adult characters in Babbitt's books—the parents in *Dick Foote and the Shark* and *Phoebe's Revolt;* Prime Minister DeCree, the King, and the other courtiers in *The Search for Delicious;* the citizens of Instep in *Kneeknock Rise;* Hercules and the Goodys in *Goody Hall*—for the most part, live happily ever after. Some unpleasantness, Babbitt argued, could exist, but it could not last: "Not without pain, not without violence, not without grief; but in the end, somehow, everything will always be all right" (Babbitt, "Happy Endings?" 159). In *Tuck Everlasting,* however, she clearly modifies her stance.

Several critics have suggested that *Tuck's* conclusion should be seen in a positive light. For example, Anita Moss has emphasized the fact that Babbitt ends the book humorously with Angus Tuck's joke about Winnie Foster's immortal toad. Moss suggests that "Babbitt has chosen to treat a potentially tragic theme; yet the fantasy is finally 'high comedy' in the sense that it ends on a note of rebirth and renewal" (Moss, "Natalie Babbitt," 24). This is only partially true, however. The toad has been preserved from harm by Winnie's action, and she, in choosing to accept her mortality, has allowed the wheel of rebirth and renewal to continue within her own family. For the Tucks, however, nothing has changed. They may, as Winnie suggests, be lovable, but they are not happy. They continue as they were, without hope, without the possibility of any rebirth or renewal. The toad may well enjoy its immortality; this is something we can never know. The Tucks, however, do not. The comedy of Winnie's immortal toad is thus muted by the ongoing tragedy of Angus and Mae Tuck. When Angus jokes about the toad that the "durn fool thing must think it's going to live forever" (*TE,* 139), he does not know that it is.

His joke, rather than being high comedy, might better be seen as gallows humor. It is clear, after all, that, although he carries the toad to safety, if he thought it would bring an end to his life, Angus Tuck would gladly lie down on the road in the toad's place. It can only be hoped that his immortality and his family's, like that of the ash tree and the tree Yggdrasil, has some limit to it.

7

Coping with Loss
The Eyes of the Amaryllis

Mrs. Goody in *Goody Hall* cannot come to terms with her childhood. Obsessed with the early poverty she experienced, she seems determined to maintain her current high standard of living despite the pain it costs her and her family. The Tucks of *Tuck Everlasting,* through no fault of their own, are similarly fixated on their past. From the moment they achieved immortality, they stopped growing, both physically and emotionally. Jesse Tuck is, essentially, a 104-year-old adolescent. It seems clear that for Natalie Babbitt our relationship to the past is the key to our ability to cope with the present. To the extent that we put our memories of past events in perspective, we are able to grow beyond them and achieve happiness. To the extent that we fail to achieve this perspective, we limit our potential for growth and set ourselves up for sorrow. Mrs. Goody is finally made to realize that the life of a poor farmer has its good points. When she agrees to leave Goody Hall and return to her husband's farm, she regains both joy and peace of mind. The Tucks, because they cannot change what has happened to them and will never come to terms with it, can never achieve peace.

In *The Eyes of the Amaryllis,* Geneva Reade is similarly fixated upon a past event, in her case the death of her sea captain husband in a shipwreck some thirty years ago. Captain Reade's ship, the Amaryllis, sank in a sudden Atlantic storm immediately off the Cape Cod shore, before the very eyes of his wife and son.[1] Geneva, now an old woman, still mourns his death. Obsessed with the belief that he will somehow send her a message from beneath the sea or beyond the grave, she refuses to leave her isolated home. Meanwhile her son George, also scarred by the incident, has moved inland to Springfield, Massachusetts. Refusing all contact with the ocean, he has seen very little of his mother and, like her, has failed to come to terms with the past. It is even implied that his mother's inability to get over her husband's death caused her to neglect him, further straining their relationship.

Owing in part to his irrational hatred of the sea and in part to his entirely legitimate concern for his mother's safety, George has wanted Geneva to move to Springfield for some time, but she has always refused. In the first chapter of *The Eyes of the Amaryllis,* she is suffering from a broken ankle, but still insists on staying on Cape Cod. George, after a final attempt to persuade his mother to return with him, agrees to let his eleven-year-old daughter, Jenny (Geneva's namesake), stay with her grandmother and help out with the housework until she has recovered.

Babbitt's choice of the name "Geneva," emphasized by its doubling, may be significant. The name reminds us of Geneva, Switzerland, which is linked to both the unbending religious doctrines of John Calvin (not to mention those of the Pilgrim fathers who settled Cape Cod) and the city's current reputation as a center of peace and civilized behavior. The name, however, originally meant either "white lady" or "white wave." The former, in Celtic tradition, was an often dangerous female fairy who, like Geneva Reade, generally lived in solitude, often in or by a body of water, as, for example, the Lady of the Lake of Arthurian tradition. The latter meaning, "white wave," would also seem applicable to the novel, both literally as a reference to the storm and figuratively as a symbol of Geneva's anger.

Geneva, however, is also thought to be a variant of Guinevere, another Arthurian connection. This should not be taken too far because, after all, Babbitt gives us no hint that Geneva was ever involved in a tragic love triangle, but there is a long tradition of

Guinevere, after the death of King Arthur, retiring to the solitude of the convent, much as Geneva Reade retires to the solitude of her lonely Cape Cod home. In some versions of the legend Guinevere, like Geneva, eventually earns a form of redemption.

The personality of the younger Geneva Reade, we are told, is very much like her grandmother's, loving, but stubborn, with a strong desire to achieve freedom and be her own person. Despite her father's warning that the sea is dangerous and the fact that she has never seen the Atlantic Ocean at close range, she is immediately and strongly attracted to it: "She watched it, amazed and faintly hypnotized, and the feeling of freedom that had come to her at first grew deeper. Wisps of her dark hair, tied back so neatly at home by her mother, blew about her face as the breeze swept past her."[2] The sea is a chaotic influence, and it appeals to Jenny just as the wild nature of the Treegap wood appealed to Winnie Foster. Like the iron fence that failed to isolate Winnie from the outside world, Jenny's father's warnings and her mother's attempt to control her hair are both ineffective. Jenny yearns for freedom from the restrictions that her family has placed upon her and sees her time on the Cape as a chance for adventure.

The girl quickly learns, however, that her grandmother does not really care about the housework or need her help getting around. That is not why she wanted Jenny with her. All of Geneva Reade's thoughts, it seems, are bent upon the nearby beach and the things that might be washed up on it. The moment Jenny steps in the house, Geneva asks her questions about what she has found during her initial walk along the shore. The old woman studies her almanac carefully, checking the tides, and listens for the distinctive sound of the tide's turning. From the hints she lets drop, it becomes clear to Jenny that for her grandmother the Cape Cod shore and adjacent waters are a magical place where "the wind almost talks" and "there almost seems to be a light . . . coming up from the bottom" (*EA*, 30). Geneva insists that "all the drowned sailors are there . . . sailing the ships forever at the bottom of the sea" (*EA*, 37).

Although she is powerfully drawn to the ocean and feels some of its magic from the very first, Jenny, like the reader, is unsure of how much to believe of what her grandmother tells her. Our instinct, of course, is to assume that Geneva Reade is deeply disturbed. Jenny's father had warned her that his might be the case. For Jenny, however, the question is irrelevant. She does not worry about her grandmother's sanity, but rather about whether her father, learning of her grandmother's odd behavior, will have her committed to a madhouse.

Jenny's first objective evidence that the supernatural is indeed involved in her grandmother's obsession occurs during her first evening on the Cape when she and Geneva meet a man trudging heavily along the shore. He seems normal enough, and neither Jenny nor the reader learn until some time later that he is actually a ghost and that no one but she and her grandmother can see him. His name, now, is Seward. When he lived, apparently, his name was Nicholas Irving. A talented artist, he carved the figurehead of Captain Reade's ship, the Amaryllis, in the exact likeness of Geneva Reade in her youth. Later, he drowned himself out of unrequited love. Now he haunts the coastline, and his name, a conflation of "seaward" and "steward," defines his actions. As Geneva explains it, "he goes for miles along the beach . . . and picks things up" (*EA*, 34). The ocean, it seems, is possessive, "taking everything, and giving nothing back" (*EA*, 36). Seward is the "guardian of the sea" (*EA*, 86), the warden of all that washes up on the shore. What he finds, he returns to the ocean. He is not, however, without pity for Geneva, who was his friend in life, and he tells her that her dead husband hopes to send her a sign of his love. Seward, though, must be true to his duty and defend the ocean's property rights, so, Geneva tells Jenny, he plans "to watch and make sure that, if a sign [is] sent, it [is] something I'd be allowed to keep" (*EA*, 86).

At the next high tide, Geneva takes her granddaughter for a walk along the shore. Unable to move quickly on her bad ankle, she sends Jenny scurrying to find anything interesting that the waves have washed up before Seward can get to it, but they meet with no success. Their scavenger hunts continue, twice a day, throughout the week. In between, Jenny explores her grandmother's house, which is itself a treasure trove of old nautical gear, memories, and souvenirs Captain Reade had brought back from distant lands. Geneva, we learn, has changed almost nothing since his death.

Then one day Isabel Owen, an old acquaintance, stops to visit, and Babbitt uses her to provide a fascinating contrast with Geneva. A well-traveled, sophisticated woman, she wears expensive clothes, is happily married, and, although in her fifties, has the manner of a woman some thirty or more years younger. Isabel obviously looks down on Geneva Reade, or perhaps pities her, for her refusal to remarry and because the older woman has been satisfied with her humble lot in life. Geneva lives almost compulsively with her most bitter memories, but she is nonetheless intensely aware of the passage of time, of how many years have gone by since her husband died. Isabel, on the other hand, acts as if she has very little past, remembering only the good parts. She tries to deny or edit out of her consciousness any memory that makes her uncomfortable. Her expensive clothes and resolutely youthful hair style, we soon realize, are all part of an attempt to ignore or minimize the passage of time, as is her claim that she is twenty-five years younger than the somewhat elderly Geneva, when, in fact, she is only twenty years younger. The older woman's insistence on a careful tabulation of how many years in the past various events occurred unnerves Isabel, who would just as soon deny that those years even existed. Eventually we discover a painful irony, that this shallow woman was the cause of Nicholas Irving's suicide. That a talented artist should kill himself out of unrequited love seems sad enough, romantic even; that he should have done it for a woman like Isabel, however, is intensely painful and anything but romantic. As Geneva insists, "It's absurd. . . . A terrible, terrible waste, and all for nothing" (*EA*, 83).

Then one morning at high tide Jenny finds washed up on the beach what appears to be the long-awaited sign from her grandfather: the figurehead of the Amaryllis, weathered and worn but still beautiful, its carved hair highlighted by "bright fragments of dark red color" (*EA*, 69). The resemblance to the Geneva Reade of years gone by remains obvious. Jenny's grandmother is overjoyed by this discovery, but it places an enormous strain on her and she develops a fever. When she recovers, she and Jenny spend several days talking about the past, making candy, and playing dress up with the clothes from an old trunk, "hats and dresses in the opulent style of the 1830's and 40's" (*EA*, 76).

The fun cannot last, however, because it has been occasioned by Geneva Reade's recovery of the figurehead from the Amaryllis and the sea wants the head back. Seward comes for it, but Geneva refuses to return it to him, telling Jenny, "I've waited too long. I'll never give it up" (*EA*, 98). Geneva is fixated on the past and on what she has lost. She has the clearness of vision to recognize for what it is Isabel's vain attempt to pretend that the years have not gone by and that she is still a youthful beauty, yet Geneva cannot come to terms with her own obsession. The figurehead, we realize, is not just a remembrance from her long dead husband. It looks like Geneva Reade in her youth, a youth Geneva abandoned on the day Captain Reade died, and it clearly symbolizes everything she has given up: youth, sexuality, the love of family, the love of friends.

Her past is gone and cannot be recovered. Geneva cannot keep the figurehead, which is, after all, not the real thing, not her real youth and beauty, but merely an image of it, an imitation, no matter how finely carved and painted. The ocean wants the figurehead back and will have it back, though it may take a hurricane to get it. This possibility does not scare Geneva. For all of her mourning and her decades-long depression, she is a tough old woman, who refuses to be frightened by even the worst the ocean can bring against her.

What can it do? . . . Rise up? Swallow ships? Wash away a town? Yes, it can do all that. It can take your life, your love, everything you have that you care for. So. What should *you* do? Run away from it, as your father did? Run to Springfield and hide in a closet so you don't have to hear it or see it, or even think of it? That doesn't make it go away. It's still here, doing what it pleases. So you stay and try to keep what's left to you. You wait it out. You

fight it and survive it. . . . Lots of storms have blown
across this bay . . . and I'm still here. Strong as ever. I'm
not afraid of it and never was. (*EA,* 102).

The storm, when it comes, seems driven by the ocean's anger
and aimed directly at Geneva Reade: "It was small, no more than
forty miles across, but deadly. . . . It paused at dawn and hung for
an hour, and then, as if its orders had been heard, its target
sighted, it veered abruptly westward toward the coast, and the
sea ran on ahead in a frenzy of excitement" (*EA,* 105–6). Though
the house stands atop a small bluff and has withstood innumer-
able storms in the past, it shivers and trembles, seemingly on the
verge of being inundated. The chimney collapses, and water begins to pour in over the door sill. This breeching of her house's
defenses finally destroys Geneva Reade's determination to resist.
The figurehead in her arms, she lurches out into the storm, apparently planning not just to return it, but to join her husband in
death beneath the waves. Jenny, risking death herself, prepares
to leave the relative safety of the house and try to rescue her.

Then, as Babbitt succinctly puts it, "a miracle": Jenny's father
appears out of nowhere. Despite his great fear of the ocean,
George's even greater love for his daughter and his mother has
caused him to brave the hurricane and come to their rescue. At
the risk of his life he "plunged out into the wind and water, and
seized Gran in the final instant, just as she sagged and was drop-
ping into the sea" (*EA,* 114).

Geneva Reade has waited thirty years for a sign of her husband's love, a message from beyond the grave. Her son, without
realizing it, has also been waiting all that time for a sign that his
mother loves him. When the figurehead of the Amaryllis washes
up on shore, Geneva thinks that her prayers have been answered.
In the end, however, she and the reader realize that the figurehead is a false message. No good man after all, living or dead,
would attempt to prove his love by giving those for whom he cares
something that would put them in danger. If she had not been so
self-absorbed, Geneva Reade would have realized that she was
surrounded by signs of her husband's love for her and his son from

the very first. Perhaps the most obvious such sign is the Captain's old watch. He had received it from his father on his twenty-first birthday and had intended to pass it on to his son, but had not lived to do so. Geneva should have given it to George on his twenty-first birthday, and she probably would have had he not been long gone from home and had she not forgotten. It is important to realize that she has not withheld the watch out of malice or resentment: she truly has forgotten it. But it has slipped her mind, in all probability, because she has been so self-absorbed, so full of her own suffering. She has not had time to realize that her son, too, is in pain. She has wanted a message from her dead husband, but it has not occurred to her that George, too, might need a sign. It is fitting that she is unable to come to terms with her husband's death until she learns to share his love, as symbolized by her willingness to pass on the watch.

A more important sign of Captain Reade's love for his wife, however, is found in his descendants: a son, who overcomes his alienation from his mother and an intense fear of the ocean in time to save her life, and a granddaughter, who seems to be everything Geneva Reade was in her youth. The figurehead from the Amaryllis may look like Geneva as a young woman, but that young woman no longer exists, and the resemblance, with its seeming promise that a return to the past is possible, is a lie. Nothing remains the same. Everyone ages and changes. Jenny, however, is real, and, through this look-alike granddaughter, Geneva can regain much of what she has lost. Jenny helps her to deal with painful memories of events decades in the past. She serves as a means of achieving reconciliation with George and of reuniting the family. Geneva Reade has her principles, of course, and she will not go skulking off to Springfield to live. The Cape is her home, and she will stay there, but she will no longer be a lonely recluse and her son will no longer be in exile. He will now spend considerable time with his mother and will rebuild her badly damaged home with his own hands.

Ultimately each of the major characters in *The Eyes of the Amaryllis* is transformed by his or her experiences. Geneva Reade has finally learned to cope with her loss by accepting it;

her husband, unlike Midas Goody, will not return. Further, she has discovered that his death does not have to mean an end to love. She now realizes that her son and granddaughter are also worthy of her regard and that, in loving them, she can most fully show her love for the departed. George Reade, too, has learned something important about love, that it can give him the power to overcome even the things he fears most. After thirty years he has also achieved reconciliation with his mother and, for that matter, with the fact of his father's death. Jenny, the least scarred, nonetheless goes through an important change. She went to the Cape a frustrated child with little understanding of the adult world or adult problems. She leaves it a rapidly maturing and insightful young woman.[3]

Natalie Babbitt emphasizes these changes with a veritable barrage of signs and symbols. Just before leaving, Jenny discovers a living, perhaps miraculous, amaryllis blossom floating on the waves. When she runs to bring it to Geneva, her grandmother comes "to meet her, striding with long, strong steps" (*EA*, 127), no longer an invalid with a cane. Unlike its relative, the Easter lily, the amaryllis blooms in the fall or at Christmas. It symbolizes not the resurrected Christ but the Christ child, representing beginnings and youthful innocence born in the dead of winter. In a very real sense, Geneva Reade, in the winter of her life, has been reborn, and this transformation has occurred under the auspices of a child. Geneva's love for her husband has been similarly transformed. No longer a dead thing, weighing her down, that love now lives in her memory, something to be shared in joy with her son and granddaughter. The living flower, and not the figurehead of dead wood, is thus its proper symbol.

As the novel comes to a close and Jenny is carried away in her father's buggy, she sees "a short, dark figure standing on the beach" (*EA*, 127), Seward presumably, but his once heavy tread now seems lighter to her, as if he too has had a burden removed from his shoulders. Jenny shouts to him and to the waves, "we're coming back!" (*EA*, 128), and then, in a kind of confirmation of her statement, finds sand in the pocket of her pinafore. The Cape, the ocean, the seashore are a part of her, and she will never be permanently separated from these things again. In the last paragraph of *The Eyes of the Amaryllis,* Jenny sees a boy cleaning up the mess left by the storm and is aware that he is staring at her with admiration. Babbitt thus closes her novel with a hint of things to come. Time cannot stand still. Not for Geneva Reade, not for George, not for Jenny. One must cope with one's losses and be aware of what one gains as the years pass.

8

A Failed Passage to Adulthood
Herbert Rowbarge

From its first appearance in 1982, editors, marketing depart-
ments, and others obsessed with fitting books into pigeon holes
have not known quite what to make of *Herbert Rowbarge*. Is it an
adolescent novel, as it has sometimes been marketed and re-
viewed, or is it a work for adults? The *New York Times* chose a
major novelist, Anne Tyler, to review the book when it first appeared, and Tyler opened her piece by stating that "someone
ought to start spreading the word that Natalie Babbitt is not only
a children's writer."[1] But the *Times* published the review in the
Children's Books section. The *Nation* chose children's writer
Norma Klein to review *Herbert Rowbarge* and published the piece
under the somewhat cutesy heading "Not for Teens Only" even
though Klein stated straightforwardly that the work is "in no
way, shape or form a book for adolescents. It is an adult novel."[2]
Babbitt herself says that she "tried very hard to make it a children's book,"[3] and she described it as such in interviews while it
was still in progress. By the spring of 1982, however, when her
article "Saying What You Think" appeared, she called the book "A
biographical novel for adults" (89). She now says, "I kept trying
to put a child observer in for the voice of *Herbert Rowbarge,*but it
just didn't work. Herbert was the one I was interested in."[4]

In some ways the book is Babbitt's most realistic novel. Unlike

The Search for Delicious and *Kneeknock Rise*, which take place in never-never lands, or *Tuck Everlasting* and *The Eyes of the Amaryllis,* which are set in real places like upstate New York and Cape Cod that are nonetheless so vaguely depicted as to be largely irrelevant to the story, *Herbert Rowbarge* is firmly grounded in the Ohio of Natalie Babbitt's youth. Real places like Cleveland, Cincinnati, and Buffalo are mentioned and visited by the characters. The main locations of the novel are only lightly disguised; Herbert's birthplace, Gaitsburg, is in reality the town of Gallipolis, Ohio, and his beloved Red Man Lake is a relocated version of the very real Indian Lake, Ohio, where Babbitt spent part of her childhood. The actual Indian Lake even has an amusement park, though it is not called the Rowbarge Pleasure Dome and is nowhere near as magnificent as Babbitt's imaginary recreation of it.

Like virtually all of Babbitt's fiction, however, *Herbert Rowbarge* has the feel of fantasy, what Anne Tyler has called "an almost folktale-like tone and plot . . . the stripped quality of a legend" (Tyler, 44). Indeed, the book draws on any number of standard folktale motifs. Its basic premise—that a young man of unknown parentage should grow up in poverty, haunted by the disturbing intuition that he has lost something important, that he is somehow mysteriously incomplete, and that he should then rise through his own efforts to wealth and fame—is clearly the stuff of legend. But Babbitt gives this material a heavily ironic twist. Herbert's unknown mother was a prostitute who abandoned him, rather than a goddess or a princess. His feeling of incompleteness is a vague memory of a twin brother from whom he was separated when three months old, rather than some intimation of a supernatural origin. Further, his success comes as the owner of an amusement park, rather than through great deeds. These mundane details, however, scarcely seem to matter. Herbert's life is in many ways high tragedy. From his first mistaken discovery of what he thinks is another boy floating in the orphanage mirror, to his eventual death, floating through the tunnel of love, there is an inevitability about Herbert Rowbarge's life that goes far beyond coincidence and has the feel of an old tale.

The novel begins with one of Babbitt's typical framing devices, a foreword in which she describes herself as Herbert Rowbarge's biographer and keys the reader in to what is central to an understanding of Herbert's character. He is first and foremost, she tells us, an ambitious man and, equally important, a man who succeeds in achieving his ambition, in doing "in life the very thing he started out to do."[5] Despite his material success, however, Herbert lives most of his life in bitterness because he feels himself to be incomplete. Although he receives love from others—his devoted childhood friend Dick, his wife Ruby, his daughters Babe and Louisa—he is unable to return it. That part of him that would have been capable of love is simply missing.

Herbert's feeling of incompleteness comes from his having been separated from his twin brother, Otto. He retains no explicit memory of that brother, indeed is not conscious that such a person even exists, but the vague, perhaps prenatal awareness of an Other so close as to be a virtual part of himself persists. This awareness manifests itself in the form of deep-seated uneasiness, a kind of unrealized attachment-separation anxiety, which Herbert feels whenever he sees himself in a mirror. When Otto was adopted, leaving Herbert behind, it was as if "a vital piece of him was wrenched away" (*HR*, 5) and, Babbitt tells us, "he . . . did not know, then, or ever afterward, that he was whole all by himself, instead of half of a single unit" (*HR*, 21). It is ironic that the frustration and anger that resulted from this separation are the very things that propel Herbert into his business career. They push him to succeed, while making it impossible for him to take much real pleasure from his success.

The first chapter of *Herbert Rowbarge* is set on 20 May 1952 and shows us the world from the viewpoint of Herbert's middle-aged twin daughters, Babe and Louisa. The second chapter jumps back to June 1880 and Herbert's birth "in a moldy room upstairs over a riverside saloon" (*HR*, 7). The book then alternates, chapter by chapter, between Babe and Louisa in 1952 and a retelling of the senior Rowbarge's life story. The daughters' chapters are all in the present tense; Herbert's are all in the past, except, that is, for the very last one, set on Memorial Day 1952, when the two plot lines merge. Abandoned by their mother on the day after their birth, Herbert and Otto are taken to an orphanage, the sort where a large original grant allowed for the construction of a magnificent and highly impractical building, but where the orphans live in considerable poverty because there is nothing left over for day-to-day expenses. Otto is adopted almost at once by the Schwimmbecks, who take him off to northern Ohio. Herbert, however, remains at the home for the rest of his childhood, unable to comprehend his loss, unable to move beyond his crisis of separation. His only friend is another orphan, Dick Festeen, an older boy who essentially adopts him as a brother. As a young child, Herbert's only toy is a worn and grubby Noah's Ark. Several of the ark's pieces are missing, and Herbert immediately takes up the "one lonely lion that had lost its twin forever" (*HR*, 32) as a symbol of his loneliness. Later, at the age of nine, when he sees his first merry-go-round, Herbert is entranced by its dazzling colors and sounds and, discovering the carousel's paired lions, is struck by how "complete" they seem. The ownership of a merry-go-round immediately becomes his dream.

Years later, Herbert talks the devoted Festeen into selling the family farm and buying just such a machine. They set it up at Red Man Lake and meet with enormous success. Eventually they build an entire amusement park, which Herbert names the Rowbarge Pleasure Dome, an idea he picks up from Samuel Taylor Coleridge's "Kubla Khan," a poem his fianceé Ruby reads him. Herbert marries Ruby, the ugly-duckling older daughter of a local Brahmin, for purely financial reasons. He pretends to love her while courting and is never openly or intentionally cruel to her after they marry, but he is really incapable of loving anyone. Although they have children, Babe and Louisa, their sex life is virtually nonexistent, and Ruby is miserable. When she dies in an accident at an early age, Herbert finds it a relief. He settles down to a life devoted to his amusement park and very little else. His daughters are raised largely through benign neglect. They grow up pleasant, unsophisticated, eager to please, and rather bovine. Neither of them marries, and, in 1952, when they are forty five, one still lives at home, while the other lives with Ruby's widowed and now elderly sister, Opal. Neither has a true place of her own.

Each alternates one month with Opal and the next with Herbert. Both their aunt and their father treat them as little more than servants.

Babbitt uses a wide variety of literary allusions to give the novel a feeling of fantasy. The three-year-old Rowbarge's initial and traumatic confrontation with a mirror is immediately preceded by a fall. "Herbert came up to [the door] like Alice to the rabbit hole, took ten steps straight ahead, and fell down the central staircase" (*HR,* 41). When he looks in the mirror he sees "another child sitting at the bottom of another staircase, and that child was wearing the same shirt and trousers and was rubbing his head, too" (*HR,* 41). In the world of the mirror, as in the world of *Alice in Wonderland,* nothing is as it seems, everything is an illusion. Throughout the book, however, Herbert feels an almost overwhelming desire to reach out to that Other whom he sees in the mirror, to go through the looking glass in an attempt to regain what he has lost. Next there is Herbert's association of himself with the lonely lion from his childhood Noah's Ark. His attachment to the lion, which he keeps on his key chain until the end of his life and which he fondles like a worry stone, emphasizes his situation as a survivor. As the lion in the Ark was borne a refugee upon the flood, so Herbert, also a refugee of sorts, was born in a room looking out over the Ohio River and would, throughout his life, as Babbitt tells us, "lean heavily on water for interest" (*HR,* 4).

Winding its way throughout the novel is a string of allusions to Coleridge's "Kubla Khan." Herbert's decision to name his amusement park after a line in the poem, although based on his innocent appreciation of the phrase "pleasure dome" and, perhaps, on the vague similarity between the landscape of the poem and that of his southern Ohio location, is fraught with symbolism. Like Herbert himself, the poem is incomplete, a fragment. Just as Coleridge was unable to bring "Kubla Khan" to completion, so Herbert can never finish building his amusement park, but must forever continue tinkering with it, adding a ride here, a pavillion there. Further, Herbert's inability to return his wife Ruby's love makes him, from her point of view, a kind of demon lover as described in Coleridge's poem, over whom she sheds many tears.

Coleridge's poem ends with the famous "vision" of himself entranced, seeking to "build that dome in air" (1.46), that is, describe it through the illusion of words. It is dangerous even to look at the poet in this state, and "all should cry, Beware! Beware! / His flashing eyes, his floating hair!" because the poet "on honeydew hath fed, / And drunk the milk of Paradise" (ll.49–54). Throughout the novel, Herbert has what appear to be variations on this experience whenever he looks in a mirror or other reflective surface. Although his initial, childhood sighting of his reflection is "a time of sweet discovery and peace" (*HR*, 42), it is also enormously seductive, and his separation from that reflection provokes rage. Throughout his life Herbert dreams of finding himself "arm in arm with the boy in the . . . mirror. They would smile at each other, and float off together into a . . . far more magical place, a dim and watery place with little boats, a warm place far away" (*HR*, 43). Even as an adult, catching sight of himself in a mirror, he is given to feeling a "twinkling sensation . . . ; it always made him giddy and confused, and unable to decide whether the feeling was terrible or sweet" (*HR*, 86). Herbert's feelings of sexuality here seem limited to a kind of infantile narcissism.

Herbert Rowbarge has occasionally been criticized by reviewers for its use of "either fate or heavy-handed coincidence."[6] Twice in the novel, Herbert passes within a few feet of his long-lost twin. In 1936 he returns to Gaitsburg out of some vague desire to retrace his roots at the home. By fate or coincidence Otto too has made the trip on the same day. We receive a clue that this is the case when Rowbarge enters a drugstore for a headache powder, and the druggist insists that this is the second time he has been in the store for the same medication in the last few hours. Later, as he drives up to the home, Herbert sees another car parked outside and decides to wait until that person is gone before entering. When the other man, who is presumably Otto, comes out, he is too far away for Herbert to recognize him, but he looks "slumped and thoughtful and, Herbert thought, a little sad (*HR*, 167). As he drives away his headlights "swept into [Herbert's] eyes, blinding him." Herbert then finds that "the loneliness of the man on the steps had touched him somehow, reminded him of his own loneliness; and suddenly he wanted badly to leave" (*HR,* 167).

What Otto learned at the home and why he evidently made no immediate attempt to contact Herbert is a mystery. Five years later, while walking in his unlighted, closed-up amusement park one evening, Herbert has an encounter in a dark ticket booth with a thief who immediately assumes that Rowbarge is in fact Otto from whom he has stolen money. Babbitt is familiar with the various twin studies that have come out of the University of Minnesota and elsewhere in recent years and is aware of the startling similarities that have been found between the life-styles of twins separated early in their lives,[7] so it is not coincidence that she chooses to have Otto make his living in the entertainment field as a cinema owner. The thief's insistence that Herbert is Otto Schwimmbeck, upsets Rowbarge, who has lately been worrying about his own sanity and who senses that he is "trapped in here with . . . something terrible!" (*HR,* 182), but he is unable to take the next step, to make the intuitive assumption that perhaps he does have a twin: "Why, there had been a time, he knew, when he'd had no name, been no one at all. His blood seemed to drain into his ankles and feet, and he feared he would faint. Instead to his horror, his face, all on its own, crumpled, and tears stung his eyes. 'I'm Herbert Rowbarge,' he whispered, but he felt that it was a lie. There was no Herbert Rowbarge. There was only this voice with its judgements—and Schwimmbeck" (*HR,* 184).

Rather than trying to unravel the mystery, Herbert attempts to eliminate the man who has placed the mystery before him. Escaping from the thief, he shouts for his security guard, not to subdue the man, but to shoot him. The possibility that the wounded man may be dead fills Rowbarge with a strange glee: " 'We got 'im,' Herbert echoed giddily. 'He kept calling me Schwimmbeck. But we got 'im' "(185). Yet he stills feels as if his very identity has been questioned. The encounter over, Herbert immediately turns on all the lights of the amusement park in an attempt to reassert his own existence as an individual., "He felt triumphant, exultant, swollen with self. He was Herbert Rowbarge, risen, and the park was his again." (*HR,* 186).

Herbert and Otto meet, again without realizing their connection, on one last fateful and fatal occasion. Herbert has suffered a series of strokes and has been ordered to bed by his doctor. The tunnel of love is scheduled to begin operation at the Pleasure Dome that day, however, and it is the owner's unvarying policy to open and be the first person to use each new ride. Dizzy, not entirely in his right mind, perhaps already dying, Herbert sneaks out of the house and drives off to his amusement park. "His vision blurs, he blinks, and sees something rushing up at him, a group of people walking in the road. He veers sharply to the right to avoid them and sees, too late, the man getting out of a car, the wide-opened door. There is a sickening thump, an explosion of glass, a screech of metal, all mixed together in a whirl. The Lincoln lurches. But keeps going. Herbert clings to the wheel. Can't stop now. Have to get to the park. Must be almost ten" (*HR*, 204). The man he has hit and killed is his brother Otto. Whether Schwimmbeck has come to the park to find his brother or merely as a tourist we will never know. He had, in any case, brought with him his grandson.

Herbert, unaware that he has killed anyone, takes his rightful place in the first boat to enter the tunnel of love. It is here that we discover the only actual fantastic or supernatural element in the novel. Years earlier Herbert had dreamed of meeting his brother in "a dim and watery place with little boats" (*HR*, 43), and this dream appears to have been precognitive. Now a meeting of sorts has occurred and Herbert, minutes later, has found himself in just such a place. Babbitt emphasizes the similarity by specifically repeating the earlier phrase, calling the tunnel of love a "dim and watery place" (*HR*, 208). Herbert, dying, sits in the boat as it leaves the tunnel, "eyes closed . . . hands palm-upward on the seat . . . face relaxed and blissful" (*HR*, 208). His posture may be that of the Buddha contemplating enlightenment. We are told, after all, that he has finally found what he has long sought— his brother: "He has floated deep into the mirror and found his only love, and they are gone" (*HR*, 208). Considering the deep line of irony that runs throughout *Herbert Rowbarge*, however, it may be worthwhile to point out that his posture is also that of the suicide, the wrist slitter. By driving himself into exhaustion and stroke, by refusing to obey his doctor's orders and stay in bed, Herbert has, in a sense, killed himself.

An issue that demands our consideration is the growth or moral development of the major characters in *Herbert Rowbarge*. Natalie Babbitt's books for children have tended to be bildungsromans; they have dealt with the maturation of their young protagonists. In the early picture books, Dick of *Dick Foote and the Shark* and Phoebe of *Phoebe's Revolt* both learn to compromise, to realize that the viewpoints of others are valid and worthy of some consideration. Gaylen in *The Search for Delicious,* Egan in *Kneeknock Rise,* Willet in *Goody Hall,* and all three major characters in *The Eyes of the Amaryllis* learn about interdependence and the necessity of loving others, even when those others turn out to be decidedly less than perfect. Egan in particular discovers the concept of situation ethics and the possibility that, under certain circumstances, a lie might be better than the truth. Winnie Foster learns a similar lesson about lying in *Tuck Everlasting.* She realizes that the rules established by society are not always morally correct and that she must sometimes look into her own heart in order to determine the right and wrong of a given situation. As mentioned before, she seems to have attained something very close to Kohlberg's sixth and highest moral stage, involving what he calls post-conventional universal ethical principles."[8]

Is *Herbert Rowbarge* a bildungsroman? Does Herbert himself grow morally during the course of the novel? Do any of the other characters show such growth? It can easily be argued that Herbert exhibits little, if any, growth and is in fact caught up in what Kohlberg calls stage 2 preconventional individualism, the belief that it is necessary to "follow . . . rules only when it is in . . . one's immediate interest . . . to meet one's own interests and needs and let . . . others do the same" (Kohlberg, 174). Not consciously aware that he either has a brother or has suffered the loss of one, he is unable to overcome the attachment-separation anxiety that is the central trauma of his life. Despite a drive to succeed, he never really develops a strong sense of his own identity. Although the love of his friend Dick Festeen humanizes him to some extent and although he does find some fulfillment in his work, Rowbarge is never capable of true intimacy and is perfectly willing to manipulate Dick to gain his own desires. He takes from Dick, from Ruby, from his daughters, but, again, although part of him would like to, he cannot give. When Dick comes back from World War I minus a leg, Herbert is upset, but his unhappiness is at least as much for himself as it is for Festeen. He says, " 'But how're we gonna manage, Dick, with you all busted up? Good lord, I'm no good at farming! I just don't see how we're gonna manage!' Despair clogged Herbert's throat" (*HR*, 72). Rowbarge cannot even properly share his own unhappiness. When, after Ruby's death, Festeen accuses him of being heartless, he responds with a rush of emotion: " 'Listen, Dick. . . . Sometimes I think there *is* something wrong with me. Oh, God, sometimes I think I'm crazy. I tried to love Ruby, I really did, but I was lonely and she couldn't . . . she never understood. Dick, you got to help me, you got to stand by me. Sometimes I get this terrible, horrible feeling that I'm only . . .' He paused, not knowing how to describe it. . . . But, abruptly, the moment had passed, the door swung shut again. Herbert turned away. 'Never mind,' he mumbled. 'Never mind' " (*HR*, 120).

What was he going to say to Dick? "I'm only . . .," what? Half a man, perhaps? Herbert actually receives any number of clues that this is indeed the case, that he has a missing part: all of his feelings connected with mirrors, the strange conversation with the druggist in Gaitsburg, the thief who insists he is Schwimmbeck. In his first unrecognized meeting with Otto, as the latter drives away from the home, Herbert is blinded momentarily by his brother's headlights and puts his hands in front of his face. It seems possible that Babbitt intends this blindness to stand as a symbol for Herbert's own inability to come to terms with his fears. Later, after he kills Otto, we are told that Schwimmbeck's face is "all cut up" (*HR*, 207). Herbert evidently hit him from behind, driving his head through the car door window. The detail is, perhaps, overly gruesome, but its symbolic usefulness seems clear. Herbert, wanting the other person in the mirror more than anything else, but at the same time terrified of finding that person, has destroyed the evidence. With Otto's face all cut up none of the locals who know Herbert will recognize the similarity. No one will ever know the truth.

Do any of the other characters in *Herbert Rowbarge* demonstrate moral growth? Dick Festeen, unlike Herbert, knew his family and was terribly hurt by their loss and particularly by the loss of his younger brother, Frank. Early in the novel, within hours of meeting him, Dick develops an almost obsessive need to please the much younger Herbert. Indeed, he quickly becomes "Herbert's slave" (*HR,* 31). This devotion, although unhealthy in some respects, does, perhaps, save Dick's life since Babbitt makes it clear that the boy's depression has been so severe that he has "not smiled since March, and his ten-year-old body, lately so rosy and strapping, was visibly dwindling" (*HR,* 30) before he met Herbert. Dick's obsession with pleasing Rowbarge lasts for years and causes him, at Herbert's demand, to give up most of his own dreams, to sell the family farm, to lie for his friend, to buy the merry-go-round, and, eventually, to finance the amusement park.

Festeen does not suffer all that badly for his actions, it should be noted, because their partnership, first in the merry-go-round and then in the amusement park, does make him a rich man. Further, he is able to create a life for himself, separate from Herbert. He marries for love and has a son, whom he names Frank after his dead brother. Perhaps because of the love of his family, he eventually becomes less dependent on Herbert's expectations and gains the ability to think for himself. Again using Kohlberg's theory of moral development, Dick moves from a need for stage three conventional mutual interpersonal expectations and relationships, that is from the need to live up to the expectations of others and to define himself as good or bad according to his ability to do so, to something very much like Kohlberg's stage six postconventional universal ethical principles (Kolhberg, 175–76). He becomes self-actualized, able to act according to his own sense of right and wrong rather than according to either what Herbert wants or what society says is proper. Though Herbert urges him to buy a big house, one more in line with his newfound wealth, Dick is quite comfortable living in the small house with which he and Rowbarge started out. With very little prompting from his son, he reactivates his dream of being a farmer, buys land, sells his half of the park to Herbert, and opens a greenhouse. When Rowbarge, who had talked Dick out of being a farmer years before, hears of his friend's plans, he responds, "Back to the farm. . . . Dick, you haven't changed at all" (*HR,* 143), and Dick agrees, but, of course, he has. In the past he denied his desire to farm in order to please his friend. Now, he acts to please himself. He does what he thinks is right, and the farm and greenhouse flourish.

Like Dick Festeen, Herbert's daughters, Babe and Louisa, also make an eventual transition from lives based on fulfilling the desires of others to something a bit more independent. For years they have lived as virtual servants to their father, and lately, to their Aunt Opal. Herbert manages to destroy the only chance either one of them has for romance or marriage. When he finds Babe kissing Dick's son, Frank, he becomes violently angry and orders her to stay away from the boy, accusing her of being "'Some kind of easy woman?' Like your mother, he almost added. Or mine, he almost let himself think" (*HR,* 141–42). Supposedly he does not want Babe marrying Frank because Frank is not good enough, is not part of the hereditary Brahmin class into which Herbert forced himself when he married Ruby. It seems more likely, however, that he would have found reason to oppose any marriage. Herbert's daughters are his, just as the merry-go-round is his, just as the amusement park is his. Having never dealt with his own attachment-separation trauma, having never really become a complete person himself, he is unable to see his daughters as anything other than extensions of himself. Babe and Louisa grow up to be pliable spinsters. Their maid, Fawn, bosses them around outrageously, telling them what they can and cannot eat, where they can and cannot sit. When Opal has her bridge club over, Babe spends the day in kitchen, making hors d'oeurves and fruit-betty bars.

Louisa and Babe, however, are not really unhappy. They spend very little time moaning over what might have been. They have their many small pleasures, muffins and conversation together at the President McKinley Tea Room, lots of nice, identical clothes, trips together to Miriam's House of Beauty for permanents, afternoons together on Red Man Lake, or at the movies. Their housework is not really very hard, and it fills the time. They still have dreams of romance and travel; Louisa, for example, wishes she were Ida Lupino and were loved by John Garfield (*HR,* 173).

Their greatest single wish, however, is to be together again. They have the very thing that Herbert most wants, most fears, and most resents; they share absolute togetherness, absolute love. Whether or not Babe and Louisa represent what Herbert and Otto would have been if they had never been separated is unclear. What is clear is that the sisters are absolutely secure. Each is there for the other. There is never the least doubt or disagreement. Indeed, it can be argued that by insisting that Babe and Louisa split up, that one of them stay home while the other lives with Aunt Opal, Herbert has actually done them a favor. By giving them a taste of the kind of separation he has known his entire life, Rowbarge causes them to be dissatisfied. Although they continue steadfast in their devotion to him and Opal, they gradually become aware of their father's shortcomings. When Babe first learns that her father has had a stroke, she feels an enormous need for her sister: "Never in the five years of their separation has she missed Louisa so much, or felt so solitary, so full of the wonder of death. The thought occurs to her that maybe, much sooner than they had supposed, she and Louisa can be together again. Shamed, she pushes the thought away, but it lights the back of her mind and she finds herself saying, in a whisper, 'He never gave a damn about us'" (*HR,* 191). When Ruby died, Herbert felt nothing, the final proof that he was truly incapable of love. When Herbert dies, his daughters claim that they do not feel anything either, but they do, and, eventually, though they do not want to admit it to each other, they give in to tears. The love they feel for their father is, perhaps, not entirely rational, but it is proof of their humanity, of their completeness as human beings.

Although they were dutiful to Herbert during his lifetime, they know that they meant very little to him, so his death is a relief of sorts. As Louisa says, "I thought the house would feel empty. You know? But it just feels like it has more . . . *air* in it somehow" (*HR*, 211). Free from their father, they are also free from both their Aunt Opal and the dictates of society. They toy with the ideas of redecorating the house, buying newfangled television sets and a convertible, taking a trip to Florida or Europe—all things that single women who have just inherited great wealth might do, all things they have been urged to do by friends and relatives. They decide, however, to stay home and not change a thing. As Babe says, "Louisa . . . we don't have to do what Walter says. Or Aunt Opal, either. From now on, we can do what *we* want" (*HR*, 215). Like Dick Festeen, like Winnie Foster in *Tuck Everlasting,* the twins have finally learned that they do not have to follow the dictates of others but, instead, can determine right and wrong for themselves. If they want to be boring, they have the right to be boring, regardless of what anyone else says. They have each other and simply do not need much of anything else.

At the beginning of this chapter I called *Herbert Rowbarge* a tragedy. Natalie Babbitt has insisted that the book has a happy ending, not just for Babe and Louisa, but for Herbert as well, saying "he finds his brother and they go off together. I know I've said that I don't believe in life after death, but . . . I see them sort of wraithlike, drifting off hand in hand."[9] When speaking of an entire life, however, unless one is assuming the existence of life after death, it seems illogical to see that life's last few seconds, the way it ends, as being innately more important than any other part of it. Herbert lived his entire life in fear and frustration. He was never a whole person. He was never able to put a name to his problem and thereby even begin to cope with it. Some of the factors involved were, of course, beyond his control. He cannot be blamed for his parentage or for his brother's early adoption. In Dick Festeen, however, he had a friend who could have helped him, who would willingly have shared the crises of growing up. In Ruby he had a wife who would have done anything for him, who yearned above all else to develop a mature sexual relationship with him. He chose not to confide in them, however, not to allow true intimacy, not to let them behind the wall he had built between himself and the world. Herbert must also bear responsibility for his last-minute decision not to visit the home, where he would, presumably, have learned of Otto's existence. Furthermore, he clearly turned a blind eye to the various clues to his brother's existence that were handed to him. To put it bluntly, Herbert Rowbarge feared discovering the reason behind his feelings of incompleteness and loneliness every bit as much as he desired to discover it, and perhaps more so.

Is *Herbert Rowbarge* in the final analysis a tragic novel? When Herbert floats out of the tunnel of love "eyes closed . . . hands palm-upward on the seat . . . face relaxed and blissful" (*HR,* 208), he is clearly at peace, but is it the peace of the transcendent who is gone on to a better existence, or, more ironically, that of the suicide whose pain is finally ended? Should we concentrate on the narrator's assurance that Herbert has "found his only love" or on the fact that "they are gone," that they are dead? Babbitt has stated that *Herbert Rowbarge* is not really a novel about twins so much as it is "about a search for a perfect mate, for the completion of self."[10] Viewed in these terms, again, Herbert's unification with his twin in death would seem to be too little too late. Few of us are as lucky as Babe and Louisa Rowbarge, few of us ever find that perfect complement, the person who makes our life complete, but most of us make do with the friends and relatives who are available to us. We outgrow our childhood traumas, we make the passage to adulthood, and we learn to cope, to live our lives with compassion and love for others, things Herbert Rowberge never learns to do.

Conclusion

Things to Come

Natalie Babbitt has never been a particularly prolific writer or illustrator. Five children's novels, one novel for adults, two short story collections, three picture books of her own, and a handful of books illustrated for others: this is not a lot of work for a nearly twenty-five-year career. Babbitt gives the impression that she sees her writing almost more as an avocation, albeit one she takes very seriously, than as a profession. She is quite frank about the fact that her family and personal life are what she considers most important. Writing is not even necessarily central to her creativity. She loves to work on projects, whether they involve writing, drawing, or carving marionettes out of balsa wood: "I think that I'm a very creative person because I like to make things. That's not a philosophical statement; it's a kinetic statement, if anything! I like to make things, but I am not motivated the way a lot of my colleagues seem to be motivated. Hurry up and write another book—when I run out of things that seem to me to be interesting to write about, I'll stop. And I'm very close to that now."[1] The idea that a writer of Babbitt's talent could run out of ideas and simply stop writing is upsetting to anyone who values her work. She is not quite done, however. There is more work for her to do.

Published in 1989, *Nellie—a Cat on Her Own* is Babbitt's first picture book since *The Something* and her first full-color picture book ever.[2] *Nellie* relates the tale of a cat marionette (a marionette that the author herself spent three weeks carving and stringing in 1987) whose owner, an old woman, dies and who is persuaded by a living cat named Big Tom to go out with him and see the world. Nellie has never previously left home and has never danced except in the hands of her old woman, but Tom convinces her that she can do both. Chewing off Nellie's strings, he places her in her dead owner's hat and drags it off by its ribbons. After several hours' journey, night falls, and, just as they reach the top of a hill, the full moon rises. Then dozens of cats appear out of the shadows. Rising up on their hind legs, they begin to dance, and Nellie, to her surprise, discovers that, while the full moon shines, she can dance with them.

The experience is an epiphany of sorts for Nellie. Afterward, faced with the chance to be dragged back down the hill by Tom in search of a new old woman to take care of her, the marionette opts instead to stay on the hilltop. Tom deposits her in a comfortable hole in a tree, which provides her with a fine view of the world around. Although she cannot move by herself, except when the moon is full, she is happy. The chance to dance on her own once a month makes everything else worthwhile.

Babbitt's watercolor illustrations for *Nellie* represent a clear advance over her previously published artwork. The author has claimed on several occasions to have a poor sense of color (Lanes, 54), but this is not at all in evidence. Indeed her subtle mixing of shifting colors to show the passage of time—various blues and violets for the sky, greens and beiges for the landscape, with no use of black whatsoever—is enormously impressive. Also successful is her use of shadow and of texture—the wood grain of the marionette, the rocks and foliage of the hillside, the fur of the cats. Babbitt spent years on the illustrations for *Nellie,* and it shows in their completeness and quantity as well as in their quality. In addition to a number of isolated drawings of the puppet and various cats scattered throughout the book, there are eleven detailed, near-full- or full-page illustrations, as well as a masterful double-page spread of Nellie, Tom, and a dozen other cats dancing beneath the full moon. Out from the book's pages leap tabby, Siamese, Persian, and marmalade cats, even a plump Maine Coon, each of them carefully differentiated and, equally impressive, none of them overly cute.

The puppet, especially the marionette, has long served as a convenient metaphor for the individual who suffers from societal restraint (see, for example, *Pinocchio* or Stravinsky's *Petrouchka*). The puppet who attempts to act on his or her own is doing something both brave and dangerous. Independent action is the only way one can achieve greatness, but it can also lead to disaster. In *Nellie—a Cat on Her Own*, Babbitt is making a point about individualism and doing one's best. If Nellie were to find another old woman, she would be safer than she will be out in the wild, and she would presumably get to dance more frequently, but her dancing would be limited. There would be strings attached; it would not be the free expression of her own soul. By choosing to dance on her own, even though it means a more dangerous existence in between dances and less actual time dancing, Nellie chooses to be her own cat, to create her own art.

Nellie—a Cat on Her Own can also be read as an allegory for a choice that many artists have to make. The more original one's work, the more satisfying it is, the harder it is to gain acceptance for it. The truly innovative author or painter will have to work harder to publish fewer books or sell fewer paintings. He or she will live without the public accolades gained by the artist who produces what is wanted, what is safe, but will achieve both personal fulfillment and the praise of those who really count, other artists. One cannot help wondering about the extent to which *Nellie—a Cat on Her Own* is an allegory for Natalie Babbitt's own career. She, too, has chosen to go her own way, publishing relatively little, writing novels that differ dramatically from the mainstream of contemporary children's literature. Even the name "Nellie" seems apropos. It sounds exactly like the kind of mispronunciation that might easily slip from the tongue of a child trying to say the name "Natalie."[3]

Babbitt, it should be briefly noted, has at least two more projects in hand at the moment. She is currently working on color illustrations for another, as yet untitled book of Valerie Worth's poetry.[4] Also, and perhaps more important, she is mulling over in her head a new novel, a book, like *Tuck Everlasting* or *The Eyes*

Illustration from *Nellie, a Cat on Her Own* by Natalie Babbitt. © 1989. *Reprinted by permission of Farrar, Straus & Giroux.*

of the Amaryllis, aimed at the eight- to twelve-year-old audience, that will continue some of the ideas about "society and money" that she worked with in *Herbert Rowbarge.* The whole thing, Babbitt insists, is very tentative, but, as she sees it, "the book will be about a little boy who is almost adopted by an enormously rich, unmarried brother and sister in order to insure their inheritance from their father."[5] After that, she has no specific plans. If an idea comes to her, fine. If not:

> Once my husband retires I'm pretty sure I probably will stop working because we'll be doing more things to-. gether. We'll be playing for a change, and I'm really looking forward to that. I would like to go on doing critical stuff to some extent, and I probably would go on doing gigs if I were invited. Patricia MacLachlan [author of *Sarah, Plain and Tall,* 1985] and I have talked for several years about starting a mail-order manuscript assessment business, though her editor and my editor don't think it's a good idea! Patty's younger than I am, but not a whole lot younger, and she works the same way I do; she only writes when she has something she really cares about, and she sees the end of that as well as I do. Who knows! We aren't ready to turn in our membership cards yet, so we'll have to see.[6]

One can only hope that Natalie Babbitt will find plenty more that she wants to write about and that she will continue to renew her membership card for years to come.

Babbitt's Place in Children's Literature

Most novelists and poets react with horror to the possibility that at some point in their career they may simply not have anything more to say. They fear the loss of something they love, as well as the loss of their livelihood. They also, I would guess, fear the loss of critical reputation that years of silence can bring. For Babbitt, however, this last possibility does not seem frightening at all. She appears to have relatively little concern for her critical reputation and says, quite frankly, that "if I'm remembered at all it will be because of *Tuck* and not because of anything that came before or will come after."[7] *Tuck Everlasting* is perceived as being Babbitt's masterpiece, although she personally prefers *Herbert Rowbarge*. *Tuck* is, in any case, far and away her most successful book from the point of view of sales and, she says, the best-selling paperback on Farrar, Straus & Giroux's list.

When asked about her reputation, Babbitt appears unsure of why her books have been so successful. She seems to believe that a significant factor has been that they are teachable in the schools: *Tuck,* for example, because it deals so well with the concepts of death and situation ethics and *The Devil's Storybook* because each story, although entertaining, concerns an ethical dilemma with which children can connect.[8] It seems likely, however, that her talent as a literary stylist and as a developer of characters has also had some bearing on this popularity.

In the late sixties and early seventies, when Babbitt was first finding her voice as a writer, literature for the older reading child and adolescent was undergoing a transformation. Ideas were changing about what was and was not fit for the young to read about. Although strongly condemned in some circles, the new realism, as practiced by Frank Bonham, Richard Peck, Judy Blume, and a host of others, was rapidly growing in acceptance becoming virtually the dominant literary mode for younger readers. Another genre, heroic fantasy, which had been around forever, but by the mid-twentieth century had generally fallen into disrepute and been relegated to the pulp magazines, also gained increased popularity with the young in the late sixties, largely as a result of the Tolkien craze on college campuses. Heroic fantasy for young readers is exemplified at its best by the books of Lloyd Alexander and Ursula K. LeGuin and at its worst by the recent, enormously popular, and seemingly endless Dragonlance series of role-playing, game-related novels. Heavily grounded in the traditions of folklore and the epic, it can be a sophisticated literary genre, but tends toward moral oversimplification, wish fulfillment endings, and the use of violence to resolve difficulties. In the sixties and seventies (and to this day, for that matter), heroic fantasy provided a radical alternative to the gritty pessimism and celebration of street smarts found in the work of the new realists.

Natalie Babbitt's fiction, however, springs from another tradition. It can best be classified as belonging to a loosely related group of books that, although differing considerably from one another, all warrant the label *pastoral fantasy.* Nineteenth-century precursors of this group of writers include Lewis Carroll, Charles Kingsley, and George MacDonald. The pastoral fantasists have tended either to create their own unique other-worldly settings or to place their stories in out-of-the-way isolation within our own world, as, for example, Babbitt does in *Tuck Everlasting,* rather than to write tales set in some fictionalized approximation of Celtic or Scandinavian mythology, as Tolkien and his imitators have done. Where the heroic fantasists prefer a large canvas upon which great deeds can be depicted, entire worlds like Tolkien's Middle Earth or LeGuin's Earthsea, the settings of pastoral fantasy have tended to be rather small-scale and circumscribed, a single garden or a house and its surrounding grounds perhaps, as in *Goody Hall,* or, at most, a very small kingdom surrounded by mountains, as in *The Search for Delicious.* Contemporary pastoral fantasists such as Babbitt, Mary Norton in *The Borrowers* (1953), Lucy Boston in her *Green Knowe* series (1955–76), A. Philippa Pearce in *Tom's Midnight Garden* (1959), and Penelope Lively in *The Ghost of Thomas Kempe* (1973) have tended to emphasize setting, humor, characterization, and moral development rather than action. Many of their books either involve some form of time travel or show an interest in the nature of time, as does Babbitt's *Tuck Everlasting.*

The work of these writers, and particularly the fiction of Natalie Babbitt, also differs radically from heroic fantasy in its attitude toward violence. Murder and accidental death do occur in pastoral fantasy, but they are never glorified. The majority of Babbitt's novels, including *Tuck, Goody Hall,* and *The Eyes of the Amaryllis,* involve the loss of at least one human life, but each individual death, deserved or undeserved, is seen for what it is:

at worst, horrifying and upsetting; at best, a necessary but regrettable part of life. In Babbitt's work the inflicting of pain is never itself painless, nor is it the pathway to success. Those who achieve great things do so primarily or exclusively by making changes in themselves rather than in the outside world, and those changes are never easy. Unlike the protagonists of all but the best heroic fantasies, Babbitt's characters, like those of Lucy Boston or Mary Norton, require moral courage much more than physical courage.

Babbitt and most of the other pastoral fantasists differ from the new realists in that they refuse to dwell on the down side of life, though it must be noted that Babbitt, in particular, is no profferer of sugar-coated medicines either. The characters in her books for children, from Willet Goody in *Goody Hall* to Winnie Foster in *Tuck Everlasting* to Geneva Reade in *The Eyes of the Amaryllis*, all suffer, all feel pain and fear and, at times, despair, but they all are able, ultimately, to cope with their problems. Early in her career Babbitt wrote that "for the children, no matter how unpromising their circumstances, it is not too late" (Babbitt, "Happy Endings?" 158). Babbitt realizes, of course, that even for the young it can be too late on occasion, that some will be lost to drugs, crime, or early death, but she also knows that children need to read about, to witness, others their own age who deal competently and successfully with complex and difficult moral issues.[9]

Natalie Babbitt does not write in ignorance of the new realism. Indeed, she is well read in the genre and has maintained close friendships with a number of writers whose work falls within that classification, most notably Norma Klein, whose novels include *Mom, the Wolf Man, and Me* (1972). Babbitt, in fact, has consciously sought to combine the sense of wonder associated with fantasy fiction with a moral complexity more typical of the new realism. Much of what she writes is pastoral fantasy, but her work is not about escape. Her particular brand of fantasy, though it may often be set in an unspecified, generally rural past, is nonetheless firmly in contact with our real world, a world where nothing comes easily and where even eleven-year-olds are faced with important decisions.

Both Gaylen in *The Search for Delicious* and Egan in *Kneeknock Rise* must come to terms with the foolishness of the adults who control their lives. Willet Goody of *Goody Hall* must deal with the fact that his parents have made serious mistakes, errors in judgment that have led to misery and, directly or indirectly, to two deaths. Jenny Reade in *The Eyes of the Amaryllis* must find a way to help her grandmother Geneva regain her sense that life is worth living and must come to terms with her own incipient adulthood. Winnie Foster of *Tuck Everlasting,* when faced with the chance for eternal life, must realize that death is not necessarily the evil that most of us think it is. She must also learn that sometimes one's own personal sense of right and wrong must supersede the law of the land. Babbitt brings all these children to life, makes us care for them, sets them tasks of considerable moral complexity, convinces us that they are capable of failing, and then shows us, with utter believability, that they, if they try their best, can succeed. In her ability to do this, and to do it as well as any contemporary children's author, lies Natalie Babbitt's triumph.

Notes and References

Chapter One

1. "Natalie Babbitt" (an unpublished autobiographical essay), 1. I am indebted for much of the information in chapter 1 to this essay provided by the author and hereafter cited in the text.
2. Natalie Babbitt, "Who Is 'The Child'?" *Horn Book* 62 (March/April 1986): 161.
3. Natalie Babbitt, "Moral Dilemmas and Doll Underwear" (unpublished speech), 2; hereafter cited in text.
4. Natalie Babbitt, letter, 29 June 1987.
5. Natalie Babbitt, letter, 15 June 1987.
6. Natalie Babbitt, "Saying What You Think," *Quarterly Journal of the Library of Congress* 39 (Spring 1982): 83.
7. Natalie Babbitt, letter, 26 August 1988.

Chapter Two

1. Natalie Babbitt, *Dick Foote and the Shark* (New York: Farrar, Straus & Giroux, 1967), 1; hereafter cited in the text as *DF.*
2. Natalie Babbitt, *Phoebe's Revolt* (New York: Farrar, Straus & Giroux, 1968), no pagination.
3. Natalie Babbitt, "Something Has to Happen," *The Lion and the Unicorn* 9 (1985): 7.

Chapter Three

1. Natalie Babbitt, *The Search for Delicious* (New York: Farrar, Straus & Giroux, 1969), 26; hereafter cited in the text as *SD.*
2. Natalie Babbitt, "The Roots of Fantasy," *The Bulletin* 12 (Spring 1986): 2.

3. Natalie Babbitt, *Kneeknock Rise* (New York: Farrar, Straus & Giroux, 1970), 7; hereafter cited in the text as *KR*.

4. Geraldine DeLuca, "Extensions of Nature: The Fantasies of Natalie Babbitt," *Lion and the Unicorn* 1 (Fall 1977): 55. For less positive interpretations of the ending of *Kneeknock Rise,* see Corinne Hirsch, "Toward Maturity: Natalie Babbitt's Initiatory Journeys," *Proceedings of the Seventh Annual Conference of the Children's Literature Association, March 1980,* ed. Pricilla A. Ord (Ann Arbor, Mich.: Children's Literature Association, 1982), 108; and Anita Moss, "Varieties of Children's Metafiction," *Studies in the Literary Imagination* 18 (Fall 1985): 84–87.

Chapter Four

1. Natalie Babbitt, *The Something* (New York: Farrar, Straus & Giroux, 1970), no pagination.

2. Anita Moss, "Natalie Babbitt," in *American Writers for Children since 1960: Fiction,* ed. Glen E. Estes, vol. 52 of *Dictionary of Literary Biography* (Detroit: Gale Research, 1986), 26.

3. "Happy Endings? Of Course, and Also Joy," in *Children and Literature: Views and Reviews,* ed. Virginia Haviland (Glenview, Ill.: Scott, Foresman, 1973), 158–59. In this essay Babbitt discusses the differences between literature written for adults and that written for children. She is willing to accept (albeit with great reservation) the pervasive gloom of most contemporary fiction for adult, but "for the children, no matter how unpromising their circumstances, it is not too late. And we who write for them, or, if you must, we whose work seems appropriate for them, are perhaps those who, far from being glum, have a particularly tenacious view of life as an experiment in possibility without compromise."

4. Kaoru Yamamoto et al., "Voices in Unison: Stressful Events in the Lives of Children in Six Countries," *Journal of Child Psychology and Psychiatry* 28 (November 1987): 857.

5. Natalie Babbitt, *Goody Hall* (New York: Farrar, Straus & Giroux, 1971), 41–42; hereafter cited in the text as *GH*.

6. Babbitt has developed a reputation for giving her characters interesting names and several writers have attempted, with varying success, to deduce the origins of those names, most notably Pricilla A. Ord in "Discovery of Delicious: Names and Naming in the Novels of Natalie Babbitt," *Literary Onomastic Studies* 11 (1984): 37–49. Frequently Babbitt takes her names from people she knows; Mott Snave, for example, comes from a friend of one of her sons, Tom Evans (Natalie Babbitt, interview, Dennis, Mass., 11 August 1987).

Chapter Five

1. Although these lines, published in 1799, are probably by Southey, the poem, sometimes titled "The Devil's Thoughts, " is actually a collaborative effort with Samuel Coleridge and appears, in slightly different versions, in the collected works of both poets. *A Choice of Robert Southey's Verse,* ed. Geoffrey Grigson (London: Faber & Faber, 1970), 79.

2. Natalie Babbitt, *The Devil's Storybook* (New York: Farrar, Straus & Giroux, 1974), 3; hereafter cited in the text as *DS*.

3. Natalie Babbitt, interview, Dennis, Mass., 11 August 1987.

4. *Bulletin of the Center for Children's Books* 28 (December 1974): 58. Babbitt has stated that, although adults like "Perfection" best, she doesn't think that children understand it very well. Interestingly enough, they seem to prefer the much criticized "The Harps of Heaven" (interview, Dennis, Mass., 11 August 1987).

5. Joyce Alpern Young, *Kirkus Reviews,* 42 (1 July 1974): 679.

6. *Bulletin of the Center for Children's Books* 28 (December 1974): 58.

7. Natalie Babbitt, *The Devil's Other Storybook* (New York: Farrar, Straus & Giroux, 1987), 8; hereafter cited in the text as *DOS*.

8. Natalie Babbitt, letter, 15 June 1987.

Chapter Six

1. The one major award that *Tuck Everlasting* did not win is the Newbery. Babbitt maintains that the judges downgraded the book for what they saw as an inconsistency in the plot. At the end of the story, the ash tree, which stands above the spring of immortality, is destroyed by lightning. Evidently the judges thought this should be impossible because, since it is watered by the spring, the tree should be immortal. Babbitt says, however, that "the destruction of the tree was simply meant to show that the present gods, whoever they may be, said, 'uh oh, there's another piece of that old religion left. Let's zap it'" (interview, Dennis, Mass., 11 August 1987).

2. Ibid.

3. *Tuck Everlasting* (New York: Farrar, Straus & Giroux, 1975), 6; hereafter cited in the text as *TE*.

4. Edith Hamilton, *Mythology* (New York: New American Library, 1953), 312.

5. Ibid., 312.

6. The myth of Aurora and Tithonus provides an exception to this belief and may serve as a gloss on *Tuck Everlasting*. According to tradition, Tithonus is granted immortality without eternal youth and thus must live on, getting older and older, until he is nothing but a mindless, babbling, and shriveled husk (ibid., 289–90).

7. For an interesting discussion of the relationship between *Tuck Everlasting* and *Peter Pan,* see Catherine M. Lynch, "Winnie Foster and Peter Pan: Facing the Dilemma of Growth," in *Proceedings of the Ninth Annual Conference of the Children's Literature Association, University of Florida, 1982,* ed. Pricilla A. Ord (Ann Arbor, Mich.: Children's Literature Association, 1983), 107–111.

8. Natalie Babbitt, interview, Dennis, Mass., 11 August 1987.

9. Ibid.

10. The potentially devastating effect of the discovery of immortality, or something approaching it, on modern society is a very common theme in science fiction. Among the more interesting examinations of this topic are Norman Spinrad's *Bug Jack Barron* (New York: Walker, 1969), Robert Silverberg's *The Book of Skulls* (New York: Scribner, 1971), and Kate Wilhelm's *Welcome Chaos* (Boston: Houghton Mifflin, 1983).

11. Babbitt, "Something Has to Happen," 7.

12. Richard Lovelace, "To Althea, from Prison," in *Cavalier Poets,* ed. Thomas Clayton (Oxford: Oxford University Press, 1978), 276.

13. Rodger W. Bybee and Robert B. Sund, *Piaget for Educators,* 2d ed. (Columbus, Ohio: Charles E. Merrill Co., 1982), 165–70.

Chapter Seven

1. Several critics have assumed that *The Eyes of the Amaryllis* is set in North or South Carolina because of a reference to the town of Greenville. Babbitt's description of the coast, however, matches up more closely with Cape Cod and, in a letter (26 August 1988) she states that "I did indeed intend *Amaryllis* to take place on the New England sea coast, but using the name Greenville is misleading, I know. It doesn't really matter except that Gran seems a typical New Englander to me."

2. Natalie Babbitt, *The Eyes of the Amaryllis* (New York: Farrar, Straus & Giroux, 1977), 18; hereafter cited in the text as *EA*.

3. In her article "Toward Maturity: Natalie Babbitt's Initiatory Journeys" Corinne Hirsch suggests that *Amaryllis,* as well as *Kneeknock Rise* and *Tuck Everlasting,* can be seen as centering on "the initiatory journey of its young protagonist, who leaves the protected world of childhood to confront a fundamental human problem" (107).

Chapter Eight

1. Anne Tyler, review of *Herbert Rowbarge, New York Times Book Review,* 14 November 1982, 44.
2. Norma Klein, review of *Herbert Rowbarge, Nation,* 12 March 1983, 312.
3. Natalie Babbitt, interview, Dennis, Mass., 11 August 1987.
4. Natalie Babbitt, interview, Dennis, Mass., 11 August 1987.
5. *Herbert Rowbarge* (New York: Farrar, Straus & Giroux, 1982), 5; hereafter cited in the text as *HR.*
6. Sally Estes, review of *Herbert Rowbarge, Booklist* 79 (1 February 1983): 719.
7. Natalie Babbitt, interview, Dennis, Mass., 11 August 1987.
8. Lawrence Kohlberg, *The Psychology of Moral Development* (New York: Harper & Row, 1984), 175–76.
9. Natalie Babbitt, interview, Dennis, Mass., 11 August 1987.
10. Selma G. Lanes, "A Talk with Natalie Babbitt," *New York Times Book Review,* 14 November 1982, 44.

Conclusion

1. Natalie Babbitt, interview, Dennis, Mass., 10 August 1987.
2. My discussion of *Nellie—a Cat on Her Own* (New York: Farrar, Straus & Giroux, 1989) is based on galleys provided by the author.
3. I am indebted to my wife, Sandra Lindow, for this idea. When I mentioned it to Babbitt she replied that "it *is* a coincidence that the cat is called Nellie. She was going to be Lily, but my editor called her Nellie by mistake . . . and we decided we liked that better. However, even Lily could be viewed as a corruption of Natalie. I realize now that the story is a kind of minute autobiography, but never saw that fact when I was writing it" (letter from the author, 22 June 1989).
4. Ibid.
5. Natalie Babbitt, interview, Dennis, Mass., 11 August 1987.
6. Ibid.
7. Ibid.
8. Ibid.
9. Ibid.

Selected Bibliography

Primary Works

Fiction

The Devil's Other Storybook. New York: Farrar, Straus & Giroux, 1987. Illustrated by the author.

The Devil's Storybook. New York: Farrar, Straus & Giroux, 1974; London: Chatto & Windus, 1977. Illustrated by the author.

Dick Foote and the Shark. New York: Farrar, Straus & Giroux, 1967. Illustrated by the author.

The Eyes of the Amaryllis. New York: Farrar, Straus & Giroux, 1977.

Goody Hall. New York: Farrar, Straus & Giroux, 1971. Illustrated by the author.

Herbert Rowbarge. New York: Farrar, Straus & Giroux, 1982.

Kneeknock Rise. New York: Farrar, Straus & Giroux, 1970. Illustrated by the author.

Nellie—a Cat on Her Own. New York: Farrar, Straus & Giroux, 1989. Illustrated by the author.

Phoebe's Revolt. New York: Farrar, Straus & Giroux, 1968. Illustrated by the author.

The Search for Delicious. New York: Farrar, Straus & Giroux, 1969; London: Chatto & Windus, 1975. Illustrated by the author.

The Something. New York: Farrar, Straus & Giroux, 1970. Illustrated by the author.

Tuck Everlasting. New York: Farrar, Straus & Giroux, 1975; Chatto & Windus, 1977.

Illustrated Books

Babbitt, Samuel Fisher. *The Forty-ninth Magician*. New York: Pantheon, 1966; Leicester: Brockhampton, 1968.

Worth, Valerie. *Curlicues: The Fortunes of Two Pug Dogs*. New York: Farrar, Straus & Giroux, 1980.

———. *More Small Poems*. New York: Farrar, Straus & Giroux, 1976.

128

———. *Small Poems.* New York: Farrar, Straus & Giroux, 1972.

———. *Small Poems Again.* New York: Farrar, Straus & Giroux, 1986.

———. *Still More Small Poems.* New York: Farrar, Straus & Giroux, 1978.

Essays

"Between Innocence and Maturity." *Horn Book* 47 (February 1972): 33–37.

"The Great American Novel for Children—and Why Not." *Horn Book* 50 (April 1974): 176–85.

"Happy Endings? Of Course, and Also Joy." In *Children and Literature: Views and Reviews,* edited by Virginia Haviland, 155–59. Glenview, Ill. Scott, Foresman, 1973. Originally published in the *New York Times Book Review,* 8 November 1970.

"How Can We Write Children's Books . . . ?" *Publishers Weekly,* 19 July 1971, 64–66.

"Metamorphosis." *Horn Book* 64 (September–October 1988): 582–91.

"Patricia MacLachlan: The Biography." *Horn Book* 62 (July–August 1986): 414–15.

"The Purposes of Fantasy." In *Children's Literature Association Proceedings. Ninth Annual Conference, Florida, 1982,* edited by Pricilla A. Ord, 22–29. Ann Arbor: Children's Literature Association, 1983.

"The Roots of Fantasy." *Bulletin* 12 (Spring 1986): 2–4.

"Saying What You Think." *Quarterly Journal of the Library of Congress* 39 (Spring 1982): 80–90.

"Something Has to Happen." *Lion and the Unicorn* 9 (1985): 7–10.

"What Makes a Book Worth Reading?" *Language Arts* 52 (October 1975): 924–27, 952.

"Who Is 'The Child'?" *Horn Book* 62 (March/April 1986), 161–66.

Secondary Works

Aippersbach, Kim. "*Tuck Everlasting* and the Tree at the Center of the World." *Children's Literature in Education* 21 (June 1990): 83–97.

Anderson, Celia Catlett. "Journey to Forever and Back: Clemens and Babbitt." In *Proceedings of the Thirteenth Annual Conference of the Children's Literature Association, University of Missouri—Kansas City, May 1986,* edited by Susan R. Gannon and Ruth Anne Thompson, 64–68. West Lafayette, Ind.: Children's Literature Association, 1988.

Bagnall, Norma. "It Was *Real* Exciting: Adults and Children Studying

Literature Together." *Children's Literature Quarterly* 12 (Fall 1987): 144–46.

Bixler, Phyllis. "Essay Review: 'Narrative Theory and Children's Literature.'" *Children's Literature in Education* 18 (March 1987): 54–62.

De Lucca, Geraldine. "Extensions of Nature: The Fantasies of Natalie Babbitt." *Lion and the Unicorn* 1 (Fall 1977): 47–70. An analysis of the conflict in Babbitt's novels between the hopefulness of childhood and the necessity for compromise of adulthood. In the tension between these two positions, De Lucca suggests, lies the reason behind Babbitt's insistence that her young characters must take responsibility for their own lives.

Hartvigsen, M. Kip, and Christen Brog Hartvigsen. "'Rough and Soft, Both at Once': Winnie Foster's Initiation in *Tuck Everlasting*." *Children's Literature in Education* 18 (Fall 1987): 176–83. Like De Lucca, the Hartvigsens concentrate on Babbitt's insistence that there are no simple solutions to moral issues.

Hirsch, Corinne. "Toward Maturity: Natalie Babbitt's Initiatory Journeys." In *Proceedings of the Seventh Annual Conference of The Children's Literature Association, Baylor University, March 1980,* edited by Pricilla A. Ord, 107–13. Ann Arbor, Mich.: Children's Literature Association, 1982. Hirsch argues that the protagonists of *Kneeknock Rise, Tuck Everlasting,* and *The Eyes of the Amaryllis* are each required to leave the protected world of childhood and take an initiatory journey that forces them to confront some basic human problem.

Lanes, Selma G. "A Talk with Natalie Babbitt." *New York Times Book Review,* 14 November 1982, 44 and 54.

Lynch, Catherine M. "Winnie Foster and Peter Pan: Facing the Dilemma of Growth." In *Proceeds of the Ninth Annual Conference of The Children's Literature Association, University of Florida, 1982,* edited by Pricilla A. Ord, 107–11. Ann Arbor: Children's Literature Association, 1983. A comparison between the decisions that face Winnie Foster of *Tuck Everlasting* and Wendy Darling in *Peter Pan.*

MacLeod, Anne S. "Natalie Babbitt." In *Twentieth-Century Children's Writers,* edited by D. L. Kirkpatrick, 61–62. New York: St. Martin's Press, 1978.

Moss, Anita. "Natalie Babbitt." In *American Writers for Children since 1960: Fiction,* edited by Glen E. Estes, 22–29, *Dictionary of Literary Biography,* vol. 52. Detroit: Gale, 1986. This is the best short introduction to Babbitt's work.

———. "Pastoral and Heroic Patterns: Their Uses in Children's Fantasy." In *The Scope of the Fantastic—Culture, Biography, Themes, Children's Literature,* edited by Robert A. Collins and Howard D. Pearce,

231–38. Westport, Conn.: Greenwood Press, 1985. In this fine essay about *The Search for Delicious* and *Tuck Everlasting,* Moss argues that Babbitt reverses the pattern typically found in fantasy literature—from pastoral to heroic setting and back—thereby creating a radically different kind of fantasy.

———. "A Second Look at Natalie Babbitt's *The Search for Delicious.*" *Horn Book* 60 (December 1984): 779–83.

———. "Varieties of Children's Metafiction." *Studies in the Literary Imagination* 18 (Fall 1985): 79–92. A discussion of children's novels in which characters themselves make up stories. Includes a valuable discussion of *Kneeknock Rise,* as well as material on other works.

Ord, Pricilla A. "Discovery of Delicious: Names and Naming in the Novels of Natalie Babbitt." *Literary Onomastic Studies* 11 (1984): 37–49.

Veglahn, Nancy. "Images of Evil: Male and Female Monsters in Heroic Fantasy." *Children's Literature* 15 (1987): 106–19. A discussion of villains and gender in Babbitt's *Tuck Everlasting,* as well as in works by George MacDonald, Madeleine L'Engle, Ursula K. LeGuin, and Susan Cooper.

Index

The Author

Michael M. Levy, a professor in the English Department at the University of Wisconsin–Stout, received his degrees from the University of Illinois and Ohio State University and his Ph.D. in 1982 from the University of Minnesota. He has published widely in the areas of science fiction, fantasy, children's literature, and seventeenth-century poetry, and his articles have appeared in a number of reference works. He is also a contributing editor of *Science Fiction and Fantasy Book Review Annual*.

Levy is married and has two children.

The Editor

Ruth K. MacDonald is a professor of English and head of the Department of English and Philosophy at Purdue University. She received her B.A. and M.A. in English from the University of Connecticut, her Ph.D in English from Rutgers University, and her M.B.A. from the University of Texas at El Paso. To Twayne's United States and English Authors series she has contributed the volumes on Louisa May Alcott, Beatrix Potter, and Dr. Seuss. She is the author of *Literature for Children in England and America, 1646–1774* (1982).